Fly RC Tips, Tricks, & Techniques

Simple Solutions from Master Modelers

PUBLISHER: Sharon Warner
EDITORS: Maplegate Media Group Editorial Staff
COPY CHIEF: Lynne Sewell
DESIGN DIRECTOR: Alan Palermo
ART DIRECTOR: Wendy Bowes
ILLUSTRATOR: David Baker
PHOTOGRAPHER: Walter Sidas (unless otherwise noted)

Published by:
Maplegate Media Group, Inc.
650 Danbury Road
Ridgefield, CT 06877 USA

www.maplegatemedia.com

Printed in China
Library of Congress Control Number: 2008932031
ISBN 978-0-9817995-1-3

FLY RC
magazine's
Tips, Tricks & Techniques

This compilation of modeling advice and how-to's includes tips and techniques as well as how-to feature articles written by the magazine's leading contributors. "Tips, Tricks & Techniques" offers you a wealth of modeling expertise in one convenient source. Designed to save you time and money and enrich your modeling experience, the chapters in this volume address modeling in the workshop, airframe construction, radio and linkage setups, electric power techniques, glow- and gas-engine essentials and flying- field tips. Packed with practical advice, this book is sure to increase your modeling fun and enhance your modeling skills.

Contents

All of us take great pride in our home workshop area and our modeling tools. According to an old saying, the real reason we get involved in modeling is to collect the tools that adorn our workshop walls and workbench—and this joke has some truth to it. But once you have your tools, how do you best organize and use them? In this chapter, you'll find many tips and techniques that will enhance your "hands on" building, maintenance and model repair activities. Two articles on model-related soldering basics are included.

SMART STORAGE

I really enjoy flying my Ultimate, but there's more to assembling it than just rubber-banding a wing on. Here's how I keep track of all the small parts I remove and replace when I rig my Ultimate for flight. I use a few short pieces of fuel tubing to hold the socket-head capscrews and their washers. I also use a section of the cardboard tube that covering film comes on to store the aileron slave struts. I cap the ends with old prescription-bottle caps.

MICRO KNIFE & HAND DRILL

I needed a short knife to work in a confined space on a new model. I took a standard no. 1 handle and cut it off with a hacksaw. The cutoff had a nice knurled section, and I immediately realized that it still had value. I drilled a $1/16$-inch hole in one end and glued the bit into the hole with a drop of CA. I now use this whenever I need to drill holes for servo screws in a new model.

KEEP TOOLS HANDY

To keep my most used tools within easy reach and off the workbench, I attached a multipurpose magnet holder—also known as a "welding magnet"—to a vertical pole. The magnets are readily available at most hardware stores and online from Harbor Freight. The rest is all shop scrap. My first attempt was a little crude: I used an old Maloney 125 as the base. My second version uses a 1-inch dowel and a few round pieces of plywood that I had lying around after my last session with the hole saw.

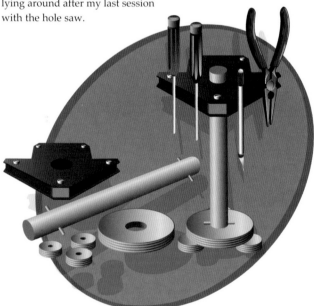

JIGSAW-BLADE CLEARANCE

The blade-clearance opening in my jigsaw's stock table is too large and makes cutting small parts difficult. I solved this problem by cutting a 6-inch square of hard plastic and sawing to the center of it. I use double-sided adhesive tape to anchor the plastic to the table, so I can remove it easily without tools when I need to change a blade or work with a larger surface. With no hole around the blade, handling smaller parts is much easier and safer, and there is much less tear-out when making cross-grain cuts.

PVC PLANE STORAGE

You can prevents your models from suffering from "hangar rash" by building a hanger to hold them off the workbench. Glue 1-inch pieces of PVC pipe together with four elbows and two Ts. Cover the wing rests with foam pipe insulation and suspend your hanger from the ceiling using $4^1/_2$-inch toggle bolts. Be sure to measure how long the down-tubes need to be for your model to clear the ceiling and how wide you want the wing rests. For larger planes, use 2-inch pipe and fittings. This is a cheap, fast way to keep your planes safe and out of the way.

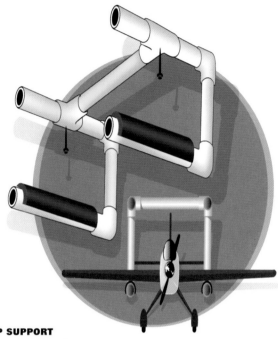

OVERHEAD SHOP SUPPORT

When I work in the shop, I often have to hang things from the ceiling—foam-cutting bows, parts I am painting, etc. To make the most universal "skyhook" system, I took two 6-foot lengths of 1-inch aluminum angle and cut a series of holes and slots of different sizes along one face of each length. On the other face, I drilled holes to line up with studs in the ceiling of the workshop. I screwed the two angle strips at 90 degrees to each other across the ceiling. Now, whenever I need to hang something up, I need only look up to find a section of aluminum angle in a convenient place.

NON-HARDENING SILICONE TUBE

Silicone sealant tends to harden inside the nozzle between uses, even when the tube is capped. Next time, pack a little petroleum jelly into the nozzle, and then replace the cap. You can use the entire tube this way without worrying about it hardening!

SHORTENING SCREWS AND BOLTS

I don't know how many times I've cut a small bolt to length by clamping it in a vise or pair of pliers and maybe using a little tape to mark where to make a cut. This approach is inaccurate at best. I finally came up with the idea to make a little jig by drilling holes in some scrap ply. Just tape pieces of the ply together to get the right thickness, and use the surface of the plywood as a guide for your cutoff wheel. This also works with bench grinders, diagonal cutters, and other similar tools, and I can usually cut all the parts I need for a project before wearing out the jig too much. The plywood holds the part securely, removing any temptation to grab a piece of hot metal with my fingers.

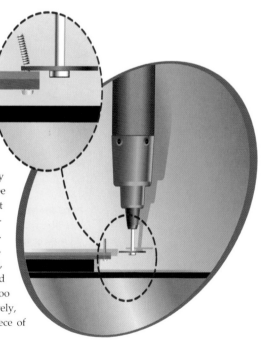

SAVE
THOSE PARTS

How many times have small parts such as screws, nuts, or washers, rolled off your workbench and got lost on the shop floor? To prevent this from happening, I lined the edge of my workbench with all the magnetic business cards everyone seems to give me. This costs nothing, and nothing has got past them so far!

SMALL PARTS STORAGE

I had a great idea while brushing my teeth. Old dental floss boxes are great for storing little screws, collets, servo arms, etc. Connect several with stick-on Velcro and label them with fine markers. The square boxes are best because the "insides" are easily removed. The round boxes will also work if you carefully pry them apart, empty them and cut a hole in the top. This is a great way to recycle all packaging.

TINTING EPOXY

I had trouble seeing where I had applied epoxy when I was sheeting foam with balsa. I added a few drops of food coloring to tint the epoxy and make it more visible. This not only lets you see where the epoxy is, but you can also see how much you have on a surface you are about to glue. Yellow is the best for blending with the color of balsa, but red, blue and green can also be used to make the epoxy more visible or complement a color on the model.

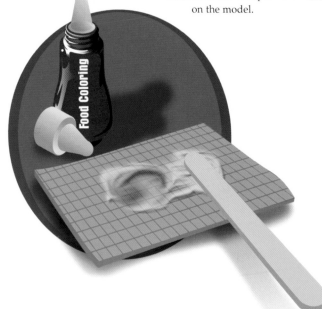

FREE SMALL-PARTS STORAGE

Don' throw away those empty snack cups. They are great for mixing epoxy, paint, etc., and for storing small parts. They are translucent, so you can see what's in them. I secure the contents with duct tape or packaging tape with a pull-tab so that I can remove it and get to the parts when I need them.

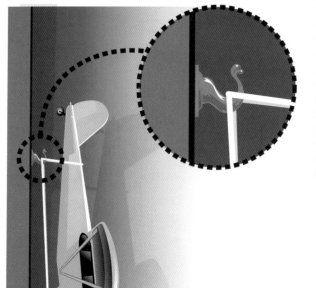

TIP-PROOF YOUR GLUE BOTTLES

Do you sometimes have difficulty keeping bottles of CA upright? This idea works well and is an economical way to keep the bottle vertical. Glue a balsa disc to the bottom of the bottle. I used Gorilla glue as the adhesive.

-----GLUE

WORKBENCH ORGANIZERS

Yogurt cups make great organizers for screwdrivers, small pliers, hobby knives and other tools. Nail a yogurt cup to your bench or a shelf, and put a second cup into the first one. This keeps things organized; tools and parts are always in the right place, and you can move the top cup and the tools next to your project if you need frequent access to them.

PLANE STORAGE

You probably have more than one model plane, and the number is likely still growing. The ceiling in my workshop is already covered with hanging models, so I expanded the storage onto the walls with this $2 solution. Screw a hardware-store hook into a stud behind the drywall. Cut a cord that is long enough to support the model by its main landing gear and put small loops on each end. Now wrap a second cord around the fuselage and back to the hook.

NON-SLIP SCREWDRIVER

Have you ever had a screwdriver slip off a standard slotted screw and ruin your finish or dent your model? Here's how to make a non-slip screwdriver. Find an aluminum, brass, or plastic tube that's a hair smaller than your screwdriver. Cut off a piece of the tube and force it onto the screwdriver tip. You may need to grind down the screwdriver with a rotary tool and use adhesive to keep the tube in place.

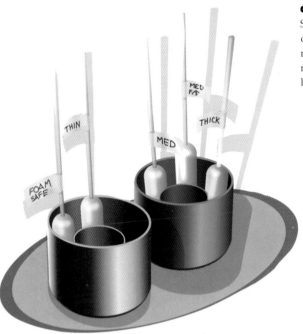

ORGANIZING GLUE BULBS

Spray-can paint caps are great for keeping bulb-type CA applicators organized. Almost all spray-paint cans have plastic caps that work nicely. I use LustreKote or Rust-Oleum caps. I label each CA bulb with masking tape to identify it for thin, foam-safe, medium, etc. With the labels and the caps, I never have to wonder which type of glue is which.

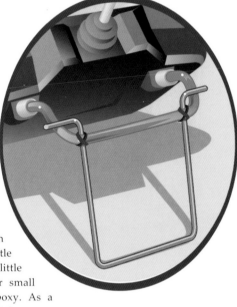

EPOXY MIXING CUPS

The red caps that are pressed into the top of a new one-gallon plastic fuel bottle make perfect little mixing cups for small quantities of epoxy. As a bonus, you can let the excess epoxy harden in the cup, and it will magically unstick itself. Just remove the excess with a small screwdriver. I stack the caps together, and I always have a reserve on hand for repairs and other projects.

SAFETY TIMER FOR ELECTRIC TOOLS

Are you tired of forgetting to unplug your soldering iron, covering iron, or hot-glue gun? Here is a solution: the Intermatico 20A 125V AC 60-minute spring-wound timer switch (item no. FD60MW) is available at most DIY stores. Plug your tools into this timer, wind it up, and know that the tools will automatically be turned off an hour later. Price? Less than $20 for peace of mind.

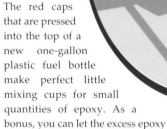

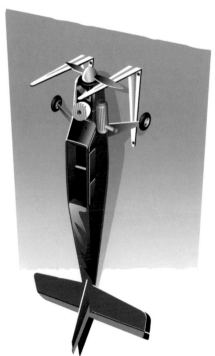

SIMPLE PLANE STORAGE

Here is a quick and inexpensive way to get your models off the floor. I screw standard shelf brackets to the wall and hang the models by their props. Glow models drip out of the mufflers, but a small twist of paper towel takes care of that. Smaller models such as 3D foamies can be stacked two or three to a bracket set.

CA UNDER GLASS

I have discovered that putting my bottle of CA underneath a tall plastic glass from the dollar store reduces tip clogging. I keep my CA under a green glass and the kicker under a red one. It prevents the kicker fumes and moisture caused by humidity from setting the CA. Try it; it works! And you can always find the CA and kicker.

RECYCLE CEREAL BOXES

Don't throw away empty cereal boxes! They are an excellent source of single-weight cardboard. I use it for many jobs in my workshop. If you harden the edges with thin CA after cutting the cardboard to shape, it makes a great template material, but most of the time, I use it for mixing and applying epoxy. The smooth surface lets you get a uniform mix, and the stiffness makes it easy to move about the workbench or hold in your hand without spilling the epoxy. I cut boxes up for templates and epoxy palettes, and I use the sides and top as squeegees.

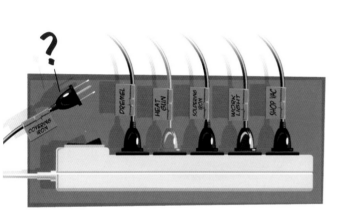

ORGANIZE ELECTRIC LEADS

If your workbench looks anything like mine, the nearest power strip is full of cords plugged in. Inevitably, I need to free a socket to plug in something else. I put flags made of silver duct tape on all my cords next to the corresponding plugs. Then I label the flags with an indelible marker so that I can quickly see what is plugged in and what I can unplug without inconvenience.

SOFT WEIGHTS HELP BUILDING

I often need another set of hands to hold a part at an odd angle or to prevent it from moving while I install a servo or do some other sort of assembly. I use two common products to achieve this goal. I bought a few 1-pound plastic bags filled with cotton rags at the hardware store. The bags are soft, and they easily conform to a wing panel or a fuselage tail boom without applying too much pressure. They are soft, so they're unlikely to damage your model. To prevent things from sliding around too much on the plastic bags, I put squares of padded shelf liner between them and the model.

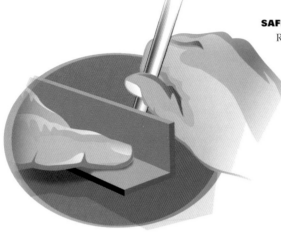

SAFER STRAIGHTEDGE

Raise your hand if you have ever cut covering or balsa using a long straightedge and paid more attention to your cutting line than to the fingers that hold the straightedge. The result may be a nice straight cut and blood on your project. To avoid that, I bought a piece of 1-inch aluminum angle stock at my local hardware store (such stock is usually 36 inches long). Put the angle stock down with one surface flat on the part being cut and the vertical part sticking up and protecting your fingers from the blade. This simple tool has worked for me for years.

RETRACTABLE WORKBENCH ARMS

Does your workbench quickly get cluttered when you work on a new project? Little pieces of hardware and miscellaneous tools all pose a hazard for your airframe parts as you work. Add these simple extension arms to your workbench and cover them with foam to keep your project safe from damage.

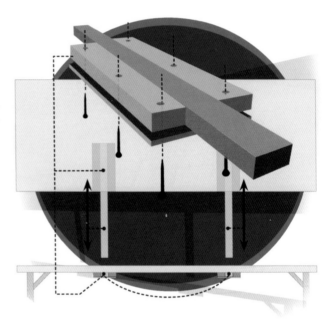

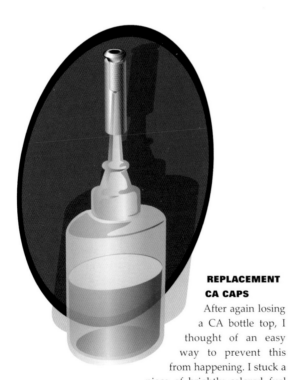

REPLACEMENT CA CAPS

After again losing a CA bottle top, I thought of an easy way to prevent this from happening. I stuck a piece of brightly colored fuel tubing on the open end of the bottle, and then I put a screw in the other end to keep moisture away from the glue. The tubing is easy to pull off when you need to glue, and I can easily find it on my hobby table.

T-PIN ORGANIZER

Here's how I organize and store my T-pins. This paperclip organizer prevents the pins from going all over the floor and workbench and makes them easily accessible (especially when sheeting). It's very economical and readily available.

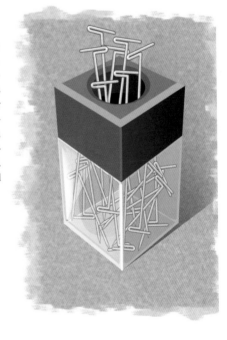

SHOE CADDY

I often need to hold airplanes steady, and many small park flyers don't have landing gear to hold them while I work on them. I hold my park flyers upright or inverted using a pair of sneakers that my daughter has grown out of. Whether I'm painting, gluing, or working on the electronics, a pair of kid's sneakers is just the right size to cradle your plane while you work on it.

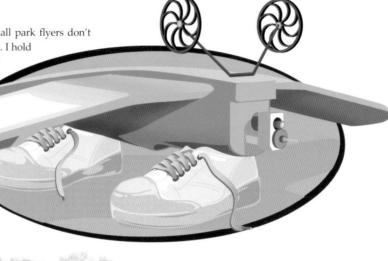

SMALL PARTS TRAY

Do you like Doritos? No? Well, buy some anyway and give them to someone who does—but keep the container. Make rails out of pine, screw them to the bottom of a shelf or workbench top and slide in the container the Doritos came in. Use the small plastic bowl (with the lid) for small parts and the tray for larger parts. You can also use it when you clean your bench. Try it. You'll like it.

WORKSHOP CRADLES

If you don't like bruising your models on the workbench, here's a simple solution. I buy inexpensive supersized clean-up sponges from a home improvement store and make the shaped cutouts I need to hold my fuselages and wings in the proper position when I work on them. The sponges are very kind to soft, painted surfaces, and they will keep your model nicely cushioned.

DOUBLE-DUTY STEEL RULER

If you stick adhesive-backed sandpaper to one side of a stiff, 6-inch steel ruler, you get a small sanding bar that's handy for detail work. When you use the ruler as a straightedge with the sandpaper side on the bottom (e.g., to cut balsa or sheet styrene), it won't slide. The ruler is also a steadier guide for measuring and marking balsa stock.

RECYCLING CD CASES

Use empty CD cases as parts containers. Cut off the spindle, invert the case, and use the bottom of it as the top of the container. They are stackable and the top locks on for transportation. They are also transparent, so you can see what you stashed inside.

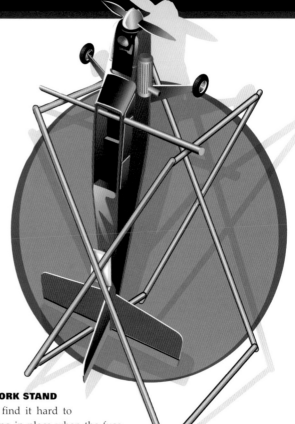

VERTICAL WORK STAND

Sometimes, I find it hard to hold everything in place when the fuselage is resting on its wheels. In some cases, it's easier to work on a plane that's vertical. Gravity can be a great third hand when you mount engine boxes, engines, or cowls. To protect the rudder, support any model with a carry-through wing-spar tube across a clothes hanging rack. I support the plane so that the turtle deck just touches the side, and I put foam between the plane and the rack. The rudder usually sticks between the legs. Tape the spar tube to the rack to prevent the aircraft from moving. This is a great way to hold the plane completely steady when you mount the engine and cowl.

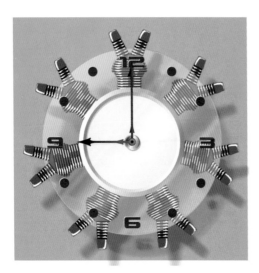

BUILD A SHOP CLOCK

While watching TV one night between scale projects, I came up with a novel idea for a clock. I started with a battery-powered mechanism from the craft store and the PT-17 radial engine from a Great Planes ARF. Carefully open the crankcase face to accept the clock and tack it into place with thin CA. I added an 1/8-inch-thick Plexiglas face and a few stick-on numbers. Now I need a light, small prop to use as a second hand.

AIR PUMP IMPROVES VISIBILITY

If you have a scroll saw that doesn't have an air pump, it can be tough to see the line you're cutting along because of the sawdust. The answer is as close as your nearest pet store or sporting goods store. I bought a "bait bucket" air pump for less than $5; it runs on a pair of "D" batteries. I attached it to my Harbor Freight saw with tubing and zipties. I needed a little more air velocity, so I soldered on a reducer made of telescoping brass tubing. I've used this regularly over the last two years, and I have yet to change the batteries.

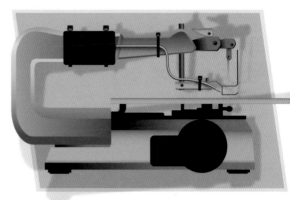

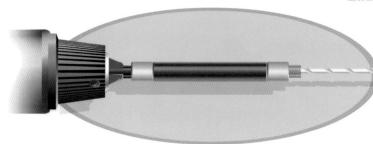

EXTENDING YOUR DRILL BITS

Have you ever tried to drill a hole in a spot where you can't get a drill? I purchased a quick-change drill bit set with $1/4$-inch hex ends on the bits at my local hardware store. It fits into a screwdriver bit extension, and I now have a $1/16$ drill bit as long as the extension. I can also add $1/4$ socket drive extensions and reach six to eight inches into tight areas. Now, I can drill mounting holes for servos and engines straight with them in place.

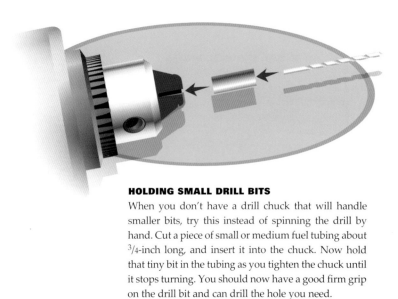

HOLDING SMALL DRILL BITS

When you don't have a drill chuck that will handle smaller bits, try this instead of spinning the drill by hand. Cut a piece of small or medium fuel tubing about $3/4$-inch long, and insert it into the chuck. Now hold that tiny bit in the tubing as you tighten the chuck until it stops turning. You should now have a good firm grip on the drill bit and can drill the hole you need.

CUT CLEANLY IN TIGHT SPACES

I routed a fuel line through my plane, and after I installed it, I realized I had forgotten to install a fuel filter. I didn't want to remove the tubing to shorten it, so I came up with the idea of using a pair of dog's nail trimmers to cut the line. It makes a nice, clean cut, and I have since used it to cut nylon pushrods, small dowels and other similar materials.

SMALL PARTS STORAGE

Labeling small plastic food containers with tape and a permanent marker is an excellent way to store the individual hardware needed for my models. I also cut up several lengths of fuel tubing and slide the smaller bolts for struts and landing gear into the ends of the tubing to hold their washers in place. This makes it much easier to keep these small parts out of the grass at the field. Include a few spares, though—just in case.

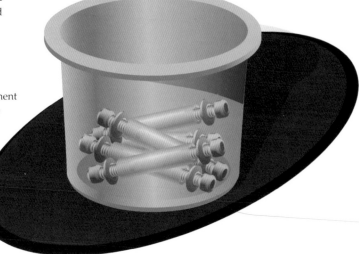

Soldering basics
You can solder like a pro

by Jason Carter

O ver my years in the hobby, I've heard many folks claim that they can't solder or they seem to find soldering intimidating. Since most of these guys regularly maintain their RC cars, planes and trucks, I've always wondered why they have a problem with soldering. After watching a few attempts, I realized that most of the problems arise when people solder incorrectly but have the right materials.

WHAT IS SOLDERING?

Soldering is a process by which two metals are joined by a third metal, or filler material, known as—you guessed it—solder. Soldering involves: heat, flux and solder. Soldering is different from welding in that when you weld two items, they actually fuse together to form one continuous component. In soldering the two pieces are also joined with a filler material, but because the filler material has a lower melting point than the two items being joined, a solder joint can later be reheated and the two pieces can be separated.

SOLDERING IRONS & GUNS

Soldering irons come in many forms and wattage ratings, and their prices range from $7 to over $100 for an iron with a temperature-controlled soldering station. Soldering guns usually have a higher power output than soldering irons. This means that they can heat a large area quickly, and that makes them better for soldering power connections.

SOLDER

There are various alloys of solder available, and each is designed for a specific application. There are two basic types of solder: 60/40 sol-

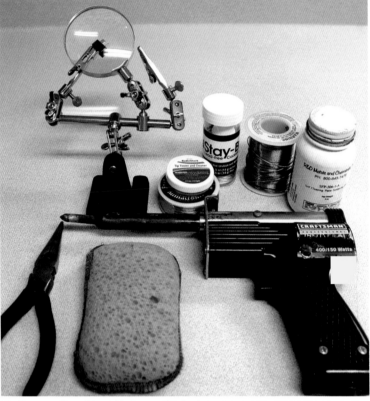

The items you'll need for soldering: a soldering iron or gun, solder that suits your application, flux (if you don't have solder with a flux core) and a damp sponge to clean your iron or gun.

der and lead-free silver solder. We'll use the 60/40 for electrical connections and the silver solder for mechanical connections. Although 60/40 solder can be found with flux embedded in its core (rosin-core solder) I like to keep a small jar of paste flux on hand.

To avoid making a cold solder joint, apply heat from one side of the joint and apply solder from the other. Molten solder will flow towards heat.

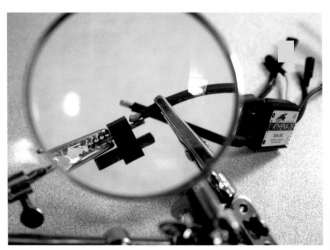

A "helping hand" tool can be useful when soldering. From holding items in place to magnifying the items to be soldered, it's indispensable.

60:40 SOLDER

60:40 solder is the most common type used for electronics work. The 60:40 designation refers to the alloy used to create the solder: 60 percent tin and 40 percent lead. This 60:40 is close to the 63:37 eutectic alloy that has great wetting and solidifying characteristics. A eutectic alloy has the lowest possible melting point, and that reduces the time that your electrical components are subjected to heat while you solder them. Use 60:40 solder only on electrical connections.

Although many of us assume that more is better, a "cold" solder joint could be hidden inside that glob of solder. Cold solder joints will eventually fail.

SILVER SOLDER

Silver solder is an alloy that contains silver. A common silver solder that's available at most hobby shops comes from the JW Harris Company and is called Sta-Brite. Sta-Brite is composed of 96 percent tin and 4 percent silver. Sta-Brite should only be used on mechanical connections.

FLUX

Flux is one of the most overlooked ingredients in a successful solder joint. We use flux when we solder to remove oxides that can form owing to the application of heat and to promote the wetting and flowing of the solder into the joint. Since these fluxes melt before the solder does, the flux cleans the area and promotes the flow of solder through the joint. The two most basic references you'll hear regarding flux will most likely be "rosin" and "acid." Use rosin flux with electrical components and acid flux on mechanical connections.

SOLDERING PREP WORK

Before you start soldering, prep your work area with your soldering equipment and gather any other tools you may need, such as needle-nose pliers, an X-Acto knife and the parts you want to solder. X-Acto sells a great little tool called X-Tra Hands. It's available both with and without a 2X and is especially useful when you solder alone. Also be sure to have a wet sponge available to clean the tip of your iron or gun.

TINNING

"Tinning" refers to coating an object with a layer of solder, whether it's the tip of the iron itself or the two parts to be soldered together. Heat and clean new irons and heat guns, and then put a little solder on the tip to tin it. When the tip of an iron has been tinned, the iron will transfer heat to the joint faster. For this reason, I always clean and re-tin the tip of my iron if it has been sitting for a while. It's much easier to solder items that have been tinned. For this reason, you should tin both items to be soldered before you join them permanently. When tinning wire, allow the solder to wick into the exposed wire but not into the wire that is covered with insulation.

APPLY HEAT & SOLDER

Here's where most folks go wrong: by applying solder incorrectly or not fully understanding how heat, flux and solder work together. Here's a basic procedure: *heat one side of the joint and apply solder from the other.* If you apply solder from the same side as you apply heat, you may inadvertently create what's known as a "cold" solder joint. It *looks* as if you've soldered the two items together, but you've just managed to melt solder over the joint without properly heating the joint and allowing the solder to adhere to the surface of items to be joined. Always heat one part and apply solder from the other. If you put flux on the parts before you solder them together, the solder will tend to flow towards the heat source.

SOLDERING SUMMARY

This isn't an in-depth look at soldering, but it should help you to understand that soldering isn't as difficult as some folks make it seem. With the proper materials, a good understanding of the soldering process and a bit of practice, you can solder virtually anything you wish. ✪

A properly soldered connection should still show the surface detail of the items that were soldered together. Cable should look like cable.

Soldering Wire Landing Gear
Easy music-wire landing gear

by Thayer Syme

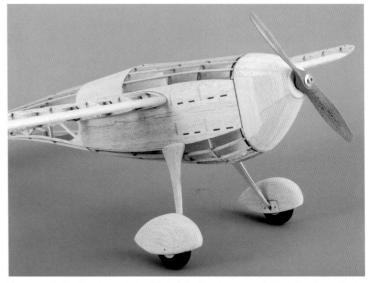

The smooth, flowing lines of the finished landing gear complement the shape of the fuselage and unify the model. A bit of covering, and I will be ready for the test flight.

Spring steel wire, also known as music wire, is one of the most popular model landing-gear materials. It is readily available at most hobby shops, inexpensive, strong and easy to form into just about any shape imaginable with common tools. Whether you are scratch-building a new design, building a kit, or just repairing the gear for your latest ARF, no modeler's skill set is complete without a few basic techniques for working with music wire.

DESIGN CONSIDERATIONS

A recent scratch-building project gave me a perfect opportunity to exploit the advantages of music-wire landing gear over aluminum and composite construction. Because the landing-gear legs for this design sweep forward, modifying an existing aluminum landing-gear blank would have meant dealing with concave angles on the front where the gear legs meet the center section. This would have meant a lot of filing to produce a cleanly finished part. I also didn't want to create a form to mold composite gear, so music wire got the nod.

My landing gear has a main leg that's bent out of $1/8$-inch wire and incorporates the axles. A second supporting leg is made of $3/32$ music wire. I bound and soldered these two pieces together near the axle. This created a triangular structure that resists any rearward motion of the gear leg but still allows it to flex outward and absorb landing stresses.

TOOLS

You will need a few basic tools for measuring, cutting and bending music wire. I use steel rulers, a Dremel tool with a fiberglass-reinforced abrasive wheel and the Stevens AeroModel wire shears. Stevens also sells K&S wire benders, as do several other vendors. For measuring and alignment, I use a sliding bevel to check angles, and I use a speed square for referencing the grid on the Great Planes Magic Magnet Building Board when I line everything up.

Last, don't forget to wear your safety glasses whenever you work with grinding or cutting tools and hot solder.

BENDING THE WIRE

The first step is to determine the bends you'll need to make to achieve the final shape you need for each of the components. A published plan or kit instructions usually gives the correct gear geometry. If you don't have a drawing or a sample to copy, I recommend that you use soft wire such as clothes-hanger wire to determine the shape before you move on to bending the harder music wire.

Getting the bends exactly where you want them can be a little tricky. I lay out the bends following measurements taken from the fuselage centerline, and I mark the wire using a permanent marker. You could clamp the wire in a vise and hit it with a hammer, but a little more finesse is worth the effort. Years ago, I bought the K&S Metals Mini Wire Bender, and it has always given me dependable service. It clamps the wire against a fixed pin and features a pivoting handle to give you the mechanical advantage you need to bend the wire.

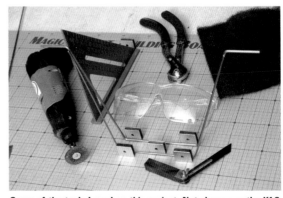

Some of the tools I used on this project. Not shown are the K&S Mini Wire Bender and the Weller soldering iron. Don't forget your safety glasses.

I like to ensure that the parts mate as precisely as possible so that the solder joint is not stressed trying to hold parts in alignment.

Carefully bind the joint using copper wire, trying for smooth wraps as shown–not a scrambled mess.

SOLDERING

If you have more than one piece of wire for the landing gear, you need to join the individual pieces. Binding the joint with copper wire and soldering is the traditional way to go, and most designers recommend the use of a very strong silver solder such as Sta-Brite. If you do not have silver solder, don't despair. I've successfully used traditional 60:40 solder for smaller models.

For satisfactory results, before you apply heat, your parts must be free of rust and other contaminants. First I wipe the wire with denatured alcohol on a paper towel to remove surface oils; then I then scuff it with a Scotch-Brite pad or fine sandpaper. I find it easiest to do a major cleaning before I bend the wire, and then, to remove any contamination that may have occurred during the forming process, I give it a final wipe-down right before I bind and solder. The last step is to apply flux to the joint to clean it chemically. The Sta-Brite flux is a liquid; carefully put a couple of drops on the joint to ensure it goes where you want it.

In addition to cleaning, the correct application of heat is critical. I use a Weller WTCPT soldering station with an 800-degree, 1/4-inch chisel tip, and I apply ample heat to the side that's opposite the part where I introduce the solder. Let the solder flow through the wire binding, and then remove the heat and let the solder cool before you move it. It is imperative that the structure be rigidly held while the solder cools. If you bump it, you will probably have to apply a little more flux and reheat it so that it cools with a smooth, shiny surface—a sure sign of a good soldering job.

After soldering the joint near the axle, I bent and soldered 0.020-inch brass sheet mounting pads between the wire legs. Your model may allow you to use nylon mounting clips. Now clean off any residual flux with a wire brush.

FINISHING

With the bending and soldering done, instead of leaving the wire gear bare, consider some sort of finish. You could paint the wire to match your model with a high-quality primer and spray paint. For this project, I added a balsa fairing because I planned to cover it with iron-on film.

I used three layers of 1/8 balsa to create the fairing, carefully fitting the central core to fill the area between the two wires. Additional strips outside the wires fill the gaps between the two outer layers. I assembled the balsa with Mercury Adhesives medium CA and then sanded it to shape. After a bit of sanding, the landing gear is ready to cover.

CONCLUSION

As you can see, there aren't any real secrets to soldering music-wire landing gear. Simply bend the parts accurately, and clean them well before you apply enough heat and the appropriate solder. With only a little practice, you will soon be able to make gear that is strong enough to prevent your model from making unintended belly landings and looks great to boot. ✪

I hold the iron at the opposite end and side of the joint from where I add the solder. By doing that, I know I have enough heat throughout the joint when the solder starts to flow. Add just enough solder to flow around the copper-wire bindings.

Left: I bent and soldered these mounting tabs between the two wires. Right: to spread the landing loads, I capture the mounting tabs under 1/8-inch plywood pads held down by socket-head capscrews.

Hold the K&S bending tool in a vise, and carefully clamp the wire under the retaining screw with your reference mark indexed against the fixed pin in the base. The bending handle slips over this fixed pin, using a second pin to bend the wire into a smooth arc.

Airplane construction is indeed both a science and an art. When stringers, hatch doors and bulkheads are properly aligned, flying surfaces are true and well-hinged and your covering is nicely done, your model becomes an object of beauty that you can be proud of. Well-constructed airplanes not only fly well but they also attract attention and admiration at the flying field. Tips from the masters as well as building, hinging and prop balancing how-to articles are included here.

JIGGING A STRAIGHT FUSELAGE

When building stick-and-tissue schoolyard-type models, I used to find it challenging to keep the fuselage sides straight while I joined them. Inspiration struck when a display of small acrylic boxes caught my eye at a local plastics store. I bought several in different sizes and filled them with pennies from my change jar. The boxes are perfectly square, and when filled with pennies, they're heavy enough to hold the fuselage sides in place as I add the cross-members.

SIMPLE LIGHTWEIGHT CLAMPS

I decided to convert my old Guillows kit to electric. When I was gluing the right side formers to the assembled left fuselage half, I needed a clamp that didn't weigh too much and was easy to use. I used two Popsicle sticks and a rubber band, as shown. Wrap the rubber band around the two sticks, clamp on one side, and then slide the other piece into place. Add a touch of CA, and that's it. To remove, slide one stick until it clears the former on the inside, and remove the clamp.

CLEANING CA FOG

After covering my wing with chrome MonoKote, I was gluing in my CA hinges on the ailerons and noticed that after the glue had set, there were glue vapor marks on the surface. Naturally I was out of debonder, and I was a little upset about this. I found out accidentally that just a little WD-40 spray on a soft cloth will remove the CA vapor marks. After gently wiping the surface, I let the WD-40 evaporate and presto! The marks had gone. It won't remove glue drips like debonder does, but at least it removes the fogging.

WING-RETAINING BOLTS

My Great Planes Extra 300 came with four $^1/_4$x20 bolts to hold the wings to the fuselage. The bolts have to be installed from inside the fuselage, but with all the electronics and smoke system installed, I could not get a screwdriver inside to tighten the bolts. My solution was to cut four 2-inch pieces out of a scrap 2-56 control rod. I then widened the slot in the bolt and glued the rod in with IC2000 CA. I installed the bolts after trimming the 2-56 rods to fit without any interference. Now I can install and tighten the bolts with one hand inside the fuselage.

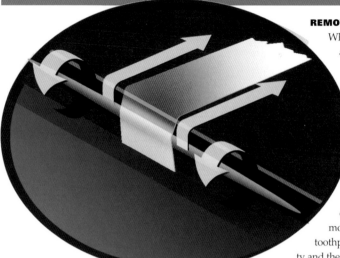

REMOVING TAPE FROM ARFS

When a new ARF model aircraft arrives at my workshop, I remove the major components from their plastic bags so that I can separate the parts that were taped together for shipping. Unfortunately, the tape often has no loose ends to start its removal. Considerable marring of the covering and sometimes damage to the surface of the model can occur. I use a round toothpick to help reduce the difficulty and the damage during tape removal. Insert the toothpick under the tape along the hinge line and rotate the toothpick so it rolls under the tape, lifting it from the covering with almost no stress. Once you lift one side, you can use the toothpick on the second side, or simply pull the tape back along itself to remove it completely.

MOUNTING PILOTS

Attaching soft pilot figures to the cockpit floor of my models was a challenge until I came up with this method. Purchase a spray can of expanding foam insulation at the local hardware store and inject the foam into the figure's head up to the shoulders. Insert a $1/4$-inch wooden dowel into the foam up to the top of the head and hold it in place until the foam hardens. Trim the base of the figure, removing all excess material to make a good seal with the cockpit floor. Drill a $1/4$-inch hole in the floor and insert the dowel, gluing to hold the figure in place.

LAMINATING OUTLINES

Laminated flying surface outlines are stronger, lighter and more warp-resistant than other construction methods. Everyone has his own tricks. Here are a couple of mine: I apply glue to all the laminations and stack them all at once, and then "wrap" them around the edge of the form. I tape one end of the stack to the form, and then I gradually pull and bend the stack around the form, taping periodically as I go. Plastic tape or plastic wrap works well to prevent the glue from sticking to the edge of the form. You can also wax the edge of the form with beeswax or crayons if you are *not* going to heat the piece to accelerate drying. The laminated piece usually ends up with some of the pieces misaligned, so I make the strips slightly wider than the piece I need to allow for some sanding. For instance, if you are making up an $1/8$-inch high piece, you should use strips that are $5/32$ or even $3/16$ wide.

BALANCING PROPS

After trying the usual techniques to balance a prop (sanding the heavy blade, or painting nail polish on or adding tape to the lighter blade), I came upon this method, which is a lot easier, cleaner, and more accurate. Use sign vinyl. Cut a small square or rectangular patch, lightly apply it to the back of the lighter blade, then check the balance. If it is too heavy, tease up one edge and trim it until you arrive at that perfect balance. Vinyl sign material has a very strong adhesion. Once applied it stays put, even on glow props! Any local sign shop should have plenty of small scraps, and they are usually happy to share some leftovers. When I have mentioned using it for RC planes, I've sometimes walked away with pieces large enough to apply as part of the color scheme—a bonus!

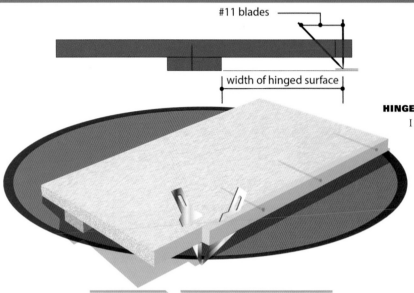

#11 blades

width of hinged surface

HINGE-CUTTING TOOL

I have come up with a way to eliminate using tape of any kind when hinging the control surfaces on foamies built using foam that's skinned on both sides with thin plastic. As you can see, the tool I created cuts a beveled slot between the fixed surface and the hinged control. For the price of a couple of X-Acto blades and some scrap balsa, you, too, can make a cutter.

CANOPY
GLUE APPLICATOR

Ever have trouble applying canopy glue when you need to get into those tight spots and use just the right amount? I use a small plastic syringe that you can buy in any pharmacy. Secure the long, thin needle cover (these snap onto the syringe), clip off the end, pour RC56 canopy glue inside the syringe and there you go. It's easy to apply a nice, even bead of glue, and the glue stays fresh if you cover the syringe tip after use!

REYNOLDS PAPER FOR PLANS

I use Reynolds Parchment Paper as a nonstick plans cover when I build. Found in the baking section of most grocery stores, it is readily available and inexpensive. It is translucent, so you can easily see the plan, and I have not found a glue that will stick to it.

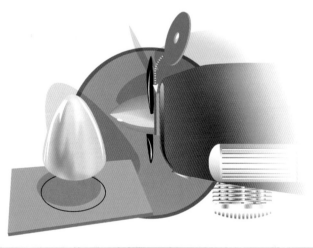

PERFECT SPINNER SPACING

Use your spinner backplate to make a circular pattern on $1/16$, $3/32$, or $1/8$-inch balsa sheet. Cut out the circle and center hole. Place the balsa circle on your engine prop shaft forward of the thrust washer, and install the spinner backplate. Move the cowl forwards until it contacts the balsa circle, and then align the cowl. You will have a perfect cowl-to-spinner gap every time!

ALUMINUM GEAR STRENGTHENER

A good way to repair or correct a soft aluminum landing gear or one that has been bent and straightened several times is to use a metal pushrod and two wheel collars. Drill a hole in the landing gear at an angle, bend the pushrod, and install the wheel collars as shown. This will also stop the airplane from bouncing on those less-than-perfect landings.

QUICK-RELEASE CANOPY/BATTERY HATCH

If you fly with LiPo batteries, you'll want to be able to remove your flight pack quickly and easily to recharge it or to inspect the pack after an unexpectedly rough landing. Here's an easy way to access the pack; it uses scrap lengths of plastic pushrods and sleeves. The outer tube sleeve fits between the fuselage walls as shown and is cut flush so that the outer canopy piece easily slides in place. The inner control rod is cut to protrude 1 inch out of each side of the fuselage, and is slid through holes in the canopy or turtle deck to secure the canopy.

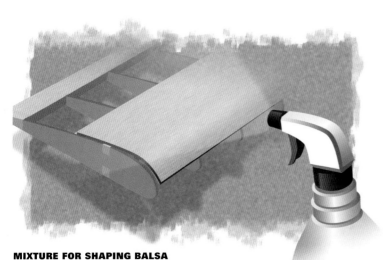

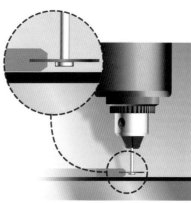

MIXTURE FOR SHAPING BALSA

When shaping sheet balsa, I use the tried-and-true method of soaking the balsa in water mixed with a little ammonia overnight. If I need to form a bend in a hurry, I pour denatured rubbing alcohol into a spray bottle and add a tablespoon of ammonia to it. The mixture penetrates and softens balsa immediately, and it dries quickly. To straighten warped surfaces, just weight or jig the misaligned piece to the proper configuration and spray. An hour later, it's dry, and much of, if not all the warp will have gone. It is great for cleanup and quickly removes epoxy from equipment.

HINGE-SLOTTING WITH A DRILL PRESS

Yes, it's *another* way to make hinge slots. I've been using a Dremel 409 cutoff disc in my drill press to do the slotting, and it sure beats any hand tools I have seen. You could also use a Dremel mini circular saw. Set the drill press quill to the exact position for the hinge slot. Place the control surface (in this case, the aileron) upside-down on the drill-press table and cut the slots. Next, flip the mating surface upside-down and cut its slots. With just a little cleanup to square the edges of the cuts, you're ready to hinge. Cutting with the parts upside-down keeps the tops of the surfaces (wing and aileron) in exact alignment.

ENLARGE THE BATTERY BAY

I recently changed the batteries on my GWS Mustang and the new battery would not slide into the molded fuselage compartment. I reviewed the manual and it tells you to modify the compartment before you join the fuse halves. Too late for that! Instead, I gently heated a putty knife with my propane torch and slipped it into the battery compartment. In about 3 seconds, I had melted the compartment to the proper size. I can't think of an easier way to do this job, and it worked like a charm.

EZ STABILIZER MARKING

Marking the stabilizer's position on your latest project with a felt marker is not ideal . The marker line is wide and may rub off or mix with the epoxy when you glue the stabilizer into place (not great on a white plane). Cleaning it with denatured alcohol can cause it to run under the cut edge of the covering film. I use masking tape instead of a marker. It makes a nice clean line to use when cutting out the covering, it helps to keep epoxy off the stabilizer, and it comes off easily when you've finished.

EASY COVERING FOR FLAT PARTS

Try this the next time you have to cover flat parts such as tail surfaces. Put the part on a clean, flat surface. Cut a piece of film slightly oversize in all dimensions and tape it to your work area using repositionable tape such as the blue 3M painters tape. Tack the film to the part and use the tape opposite your iron to tension the film and eliminate wrinkles. Apply the iron to secure the covering to the part, and then trim the film and secure the edges. This technique will keep parts such as elevators and rudders perfectly flat as you shrink the film.

PROTECT YOUR MODEL'S BELLY

This idea will protect the underside of a fuselage from getting banged up when landing on rough surfaces. Apply a simple peel-and-stick picture hanger to the underside of your model just ahead of the CG. These hooks are available at any hardware store and can even double as a towhook for a small glider if you epoxy it into place.

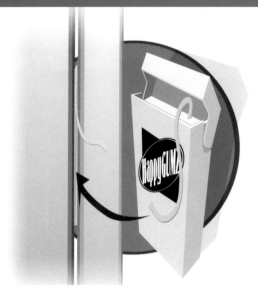

PAINT-FREE HINGES

When you have to install the control surfaces before completing the final painting, there's an easy way to keep paint off the hinges. Wrap several turns of waxed dental floss around each hinge before you start painting. When the paint has dried, remove the floss and you'll have a paint-free hinge.

CRAYOLA HINGES

There is a simple, foolproof way to ensure that the next time you install CA hinges, the control surface will work smoothly with very little gap and no glue to pick out of the hinges. Draw a line down the centerline of each hinge with a pencil, and then rub a crayon along the hinge line. The wax from the crayon will ensure no CA will glue the movable parts together, yet the hinges have enough wicking power to easily pull the CA into the hinge slot. Pick a color close to your final covering choice, or just use something easy to see. This also helps you center the hinges between the two surfaces and works like a charm!

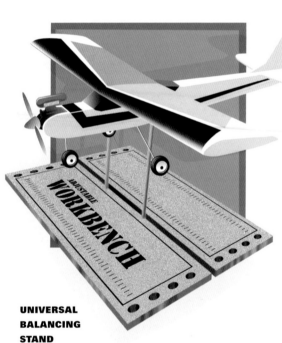

UNIVERSAL BALANCING STAND

I have rigged up several CG stands to fit various aircraft, but I recently discovered that I had the perfect universal stand and had just not thought to use it. Any of you with a Black & Decker Workmate (or equivalent) stand may wish to try this. Cut two dowel rods approximately 18 inches long, and equip one end of each with a removable eraser. Clamp the rods vertically, spaced slightly apart as required and of a height to accommodate your airplane. On smaller models, I just use two wooden pencils with erasers. This works great and is truly universal.

GETTING IT REALLY FLAT

When sanding large, flat areas such as the bottom of a wing or built-up aileron, it is important to keep the surfaces smooth and even. Instead of hand holding a folded piece of sandpaper or using a sanding block, I use some spray adhesive to attach a full sheet of sandpaper to a flat surface like plywood or a laminated shelf. I move the object to be sanded across the surface to create a finished part that is uniform.

PERFECT TAPE HINGING

Attach aileron hinge tape to the upper and lower sides of a wing's hinge joint as follows: put the wing on the edge of your workbench and, if necessary, secure it to the bench with masking tape. Turn the aileron upside-down, and position it on the wing so that its leading edge is perfectly aligned with the wing's trailing edge in the aileron bay. Center the aileron side

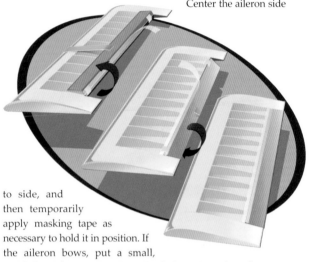

to side, and then temporarily apply masking tape as necessary to hold it in position. If the aileron bows, put a small, padded weight on it. Run the strip of aileron tape along the middle of the joint, and carefully smooth it down to ensure a good bond. Rotate the aileron to its full downward deflection, and anchor it with a piece of masking tape. Apply the hinge tape to the top surface of the hinge joint. You now have a perfectly aligned and sealed tape hinge.

WING-TUBE SECURITY

Most of my models have a two-piece wing. Each wing half slides onto a wing tube that's mounted in the fuselage. I've found that the wing tube can slide a little when you install the wings, and the lengths of tube in each wing half won't be equal. To prevent this, I first center the wing tube. Next, I drill a 1/16-inch hole through the tube receiver inside the fuselage and directly through the wing tube. Then I screw a no. 2 servo mounting screw (with attached washer) into the hole. The wing tube is now permanently centered and will not move. To ensure maximum strength, be sure to drill into the side of the tube and not into the top or bottom surface.

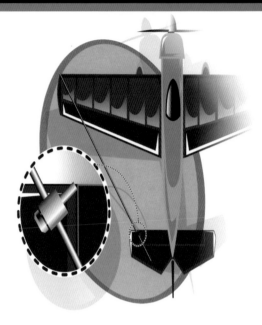

ALIGN YOUR MODEL

An easy way to align the horizontal tail and the wing is to use a 0.070-inch carbon-fiber rod with a spare Du-Bro EZ connector attached to it to be used as a marker. When I have the two sides equidistant, the tightened connector allows me to recheck each side or final-glue later. The EZ marker doesn't slide as tape does, and the carbon-fiber rod ensures a straight line. Spare music wire could also be used for the same purpose.

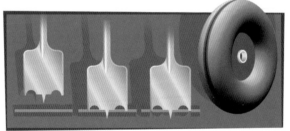

MAKE LIGHTWEIGHT WHEELS

Frustrated by a shortage of cheap light wheels that could take a lot of hard landings, I decided to make my own as follows:

■ Laminate a sheet of 1/32 ply between two sheets of 1/8 balsa.

■ Modify a spade bit with a chainsaw file as shown.

■ Set your drill press to its high speed, and drill halfway through the laminated sheet.

■ Turn the sheet over and reverse the process.

■ Thread the wheels onto a length of plastic tubing smeared with adhesive. Insert a razor blade between the wheel pairs when the adhesive is dry, and roll to and fro to part them. Paint to suit. I use an ink pad loaded with real auto tire paint.

Once you've set everything up, making a wheel takes only a minute or so. I have never had to replace one of these wheels in the three years that I have used this technique.

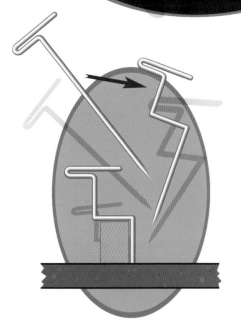

SIMPLE TAILWHEEL

Here is a simple way to make a small light tailwheel. I started making them for some of my electrics for which I wanted a tailwheel instead of a skid. I make them using a small piece of $1/4$-inch dowel, a $1/4$-inch-i.d. grommet and a little CA. If you want to get really fancy, you can roll an O-ring into the groove of the grommet.

Editors' note: of course, small tailwheels are commercially available from Du-Bro and other companies, but they do not show "the hand" of the modeler. Such a tailwheel would be ideal on an old-timer design, one from an era before instant gratification became the norm.

QUIET WHEELS

If you don't like the noisy landings and takeoffs that you get with the plastic wheels supplied with some of the small kits, there's a way to quiet things. Go to your local bicycle shop and scrounge an old bicycle inner tube. Cut rings of the appropriate size to fit over the plastic wheels like a tire. A small spot of CA will hold them in place. All sizes of inner tubes are available, and the "tire" can easily be replaced when it's worn. If you fly off hard surfaces such as concrete or asphalt, you can use this tip to lengthen the life of rubber tires.

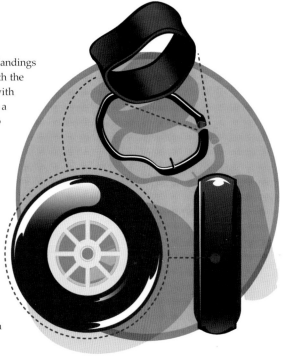

PIN CLAMPS

When we build, we sometimes pin parts down on the plans to hold them, but this is not as easy as it sounds. Pinning through a wooden part may split it, and spruce or basswood is often too hard to push the pin through without a hammer. Cross-pinning has a tendency to shift the part out of position. My solution is to take a pin of any size and squeeze it in my Z-bend pliers. The resulting shape does not actually go through the wood, but instead clamps it to the building board.

LEGO BUILDING JIG

When you glue stabs on or align wing-mounting shoulders or other parts of a small aircraft, it's essential that the right and left sides be equidistant from the tabletop or building board. Lego building blocks can help you to ensure this, and you can use them to hold your aircraft in place while you work on it. Lego building surfaces with molded pegs are also available to hold your homemade Lego jigs in position.

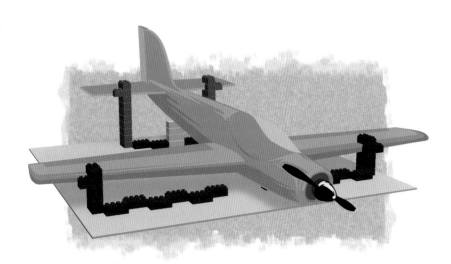

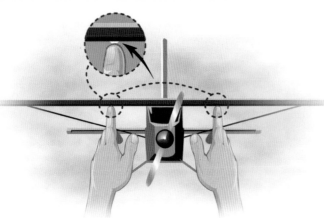

CHECK BALANCE BY FEEL

I check the CG on my models easily and reliably at the field. Instead of just using a pen to mark the underside of the wing, I use a few small drops of CA at the recommended CG location. You can easily feel the dots and position your fingers for a quick field check without having to lift the model and look under the wing.

INK REFILL GLUE DISPENSER

I use white PVA woodworking glue for a lot of my model building, and the large bottles are awkward to use and often deliver more glue than I need. To solve this problem, I use a small bottle that comes in an inkjet-printer refill kit. It can deliver a precise amount of glue and reach into confined areas, and it has a slip-on rubber cap to seal the nozzle. As a bonus, it can also be used to simulate rivets by depositing tiny dots of glue on a surface. If the bottle is not thoroughly cleaned, the glue takes on the color of the ink previously contained, and this may be helpful to show where glue has dried.

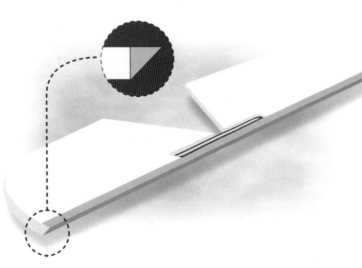

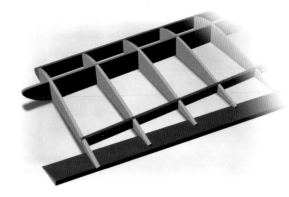

HINGING SHEET-FOAM CONTROL SURFACES

Most instructions for foamies suggest either that you cut or sand a bevel on the edge of the control-surface leading edge. When you do this, you may get a jagged knife-edge. Here is a simple solution that greatly increases accuracy and stiffness while adding very little weight. I'll describe my method using a $^1/4$-inch-thick aileron as an example. Cut a $^1/4$-inch wide strip off the aileron's leading edge, cutting at 90 degrees to the surface. Put the aileron down on a wax-paper-covered flat surface, and weight it down to ensure flatness and straightness. Cut and glue a strip of $^1/4$-inch balsa triangle stock to the aileron using epoxy or foam-safe CA. I put a bead of foam-safe CA on the foam aileron, spray the triangle with accelerator and then put the triangle on the foam. The balsa triangle also strengthens the part, and it does away with shredded knife edges. 3M Scotch Stretchy tape is a good hinge tape; it does not tear and is very sticky. It is available in $^3/16$-inch-wide, 300-inch-long rolls. It also makes a good wing leading-edge protector for foamies.

ESTABLISH ACCURATE WASHOUT

Unless you use a totally symmetrical airfoil, it is a good idea to build washout into a model's wingtips to improve its stall characteristics. Adding washout by decreasing the airfoil's angle of attack delays the stall at the wingtip so that the main wing section stalls first. I use pre-formed aileron stock as a shim. Slide the tapered edge under the back of the ribs at an angle before the final glue-up. You'll have a gradual washout that can be duplicated evenly on both sides. Slide the wingtip end of the tapered aileron stock farther under the ribs as it approaches the tip to produce gradual, accurate washout. Mark the aileron stock to reference the ribs on the side you did first so that you'll be able to accurately duplicate it on the opposite wingtip.

FOAM-RUBBER CLAMPS

Clamping parts inside a fuselage can be challenging when building a new model—even more so with an ARF, since you are usually starting with a completed fuselage. Blocks of foam rubber come in handy here. For instance, when you glue a shrink-wrapped servo into your next park flyer, wedge a block of foam rubber between the servo and the opposite fuselage side while the epoxy is curing. The foam will provide just enough push to hold the servo in place but not enough to damage anything.

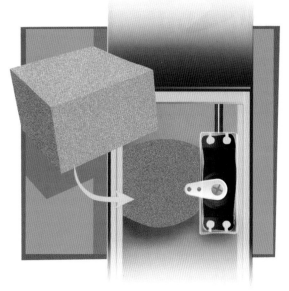

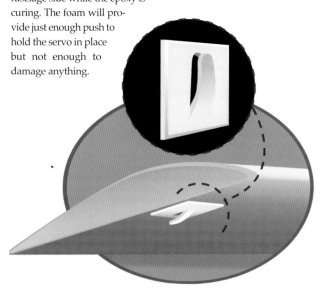

PROTECT YOUR TIPS

RC student pilots have more than their fair share of wingtip scrapes and damage while learning to land. My models' wingtips always needed recovering. Fortunately, there's a lightweight and inexpensive solution. At the hardware store, I came across 1x1-inch square plastic picture hangers that only weigh about 1 gram each. Stick one hook under each tip to protect the wings from the ground on less than perfect landings. Since they just stick in place, they are easy to replace at the field if necessary, but they can withstand many scrapes before needing replacement. At less than $2 for eight, they are also very affordable.

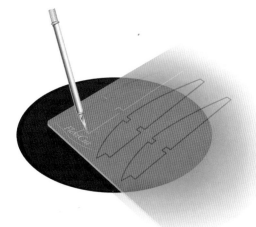

INEXPENSIVE
TRANSPARENT TEMPLATE STOCK

The next time you are in the local dollar store, pick up a pack of disposable cutting boards. They are sufficiently cut-resistant to protect your plans and building board, but they are also transparent enough to draw part outlines on them. You can then cut out the shape with scissors. The material is flexible but rigid enough to make very useful templates for marking and cutting parts when you scratch-build or repair a kit or an ARF.

REGLUE
THAT WING
SHEETING

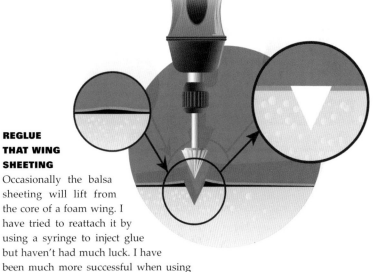

Occasionally the balsa sheeting will lift from the core of a foam wing. I have tried to reattach it by using a syringe to inject glue but haven't had much luck. I have been much more successful when using the following technique. I use a rotary tool with a tapered cutter to create a number of conical holes through the sheeting and into the foam. Then I use foam-safe CA to attach the loose sheeting. The glue forms a rivet as it cures. I then fill the voids with lightweight spackle and sand it smooth again. After covering, the repair is invisible and very strong.

Make Unlimited Throw Hinges
Gapless, strong & easy to make

by David Baron

Unlimited-throw hinges are easy to make by sewing Kevlar cord through the trailing edge of a wing and the leading edge of its adjoining control surface. Sewn hinges are widely used on highly maneuverable 3D ships because they are very strong and allow control surfaces to rotate as much as you want them to. They also work well on sport airplanes.

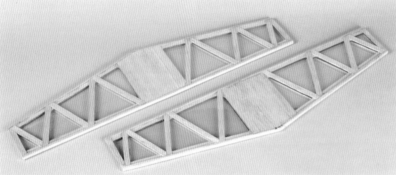

2 Both surfaces should be covered with film before sewn hinges are installed. In this example, a fun-fly airplane's stabilizer and elevator will be hinged.

3 Kevlar cord is widely available in various thicknesses from companies such as Aerospace Composite Products and Sullivan Products. (This cord is from a Sullivan "pull-pull" rigging package.) Anything from fishing line to fine string will work well. Cut an 18-inch length of Kevlar cord using a sharp, single-edge razor blade. This is enough cord for about two hinges.

6 Knot the back end of the Kevlar cord and then pull it through the first hole until the knot snugs into the hole.

7 The knot should be just large enough not to slip through the hole.

8 Put CA on the knot so that it wicks into the hole and anchors the string to the balsa. Apply the CA sparingly. I used Bob Smith Industries thin. The length of cord that protrudes from the other side of the stab, opposite the knot, is pulled around the trailing edge of the stabilizer, up through the hinge joint and then down into the hole that is directly opposite on the leading edge of the elevator.

9 Move the cord in figure-8s through all the holes, and lace the wing and control surface together much as you lace shoes.

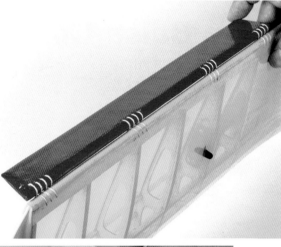

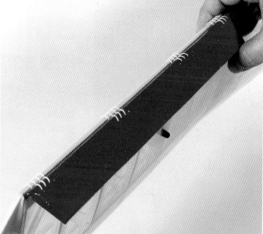

1 Note how the control surface literally rolls around the radius of the wing's trailing edge as it rotates. For maximum rotation, the abutting wing and control-surface edges should have circular cross-sections. This hinge technique also works well with other trailing and leading edge cross-section shapes e.g., flat and circular.

4 To space the hinge threads evenly, mark points on the leading and trailing edges where you will drill through the wood. The holes should be about $1/8$ inch apart and should be drilled directly across from one another on each surface. Hinges often have four, five or six holes on each surface—your choice.

5 Drill through the balsa frame with a small-diameter bit.

10 As you pull the cord through the hole, the slack is pulled into the hinge joint.

11 Once the cord has been laced through all the holes and the slack has been eliminated, it is important to center the stab and elevator trailing and leading edges before you anchor the cord with CA.

12 When you've centered the two surfaces, pull the free end of the protruding cord so that it snugs tightly through all the holes in the joint. Put a small drop of CA into the hole where it exits to anchor it in place in the balsa frame.

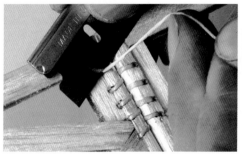

13 Trim off the excess cord that has been CA'd and also trim the short piece that protrudes from the knotted side where the cord was first inserted.

14 Wick a little CA into each hole so that the cord is firmly held in wherever it passes through the balsa frame. Do not put CA on any part of the external loops of Kevlar.

15 This fully hinged stab and elevator tail piece is ready to be installed on a fun-fly ship. The hinges will probably outlast everything else on the plane!

Building a Balsa Cowl
It's easier than you think

by Thayer Syme

Even in today's world of ARFs, modelers still enjoy creating their own aircraft. Many of these projects require a little creativity to enclose the powerplant. It may seem old-fashioned to build a cowl out of balsa, but there are several very compelling reasons to do so. The most obvious is that balsa is light, strong, readily available and easy to shape. Yes, you will make a bit of a mess, but a shop-vac will make quick work of the cleanup. And if your model is electric-powered, you won't need to bother about messy fuelproofing.

One great appeal of balsa cowls is that they can be finished with the same process as is used on the rest of the model. This gives a perfect—yes, actually perfect; not just close—color match with the fuselage.

The first thing you will need is wood. I mail-order my balsa in bulk from suppliers such as Balsa USA and SIG, and I regularly save the larger scraps that look as if they will be useful later. This is a perfect project for clearing scrap out of your scrap box.

1 The subject model is my 150% Daddy-O powered by a Hacker A30-16M. I designed the model with a 3.5-inch dimension between the forward bulkhead and the forward cowl edge to accommodate a wide range of possible motors. The Hacker is quite short, so I mounted it with nylon and dowel standoffs and an 1/8-inch birch plywood intermediary union ring. I also cut a 1/16-inch plywood rear cowl ring to match the forward bulkhead. Two dowel pins and four rare-earth magnets position and hold the cowl in place.

2 I cut an 1/8-inch plywood disc and backed it with a 1/4-inch ring of balsa to establish the front of the cowl. Next, I added scrap balsa sheet to rough in the cowl cheeks and a center keel to the chin area to guide the final shape. I used thin Zap CA for all construction.

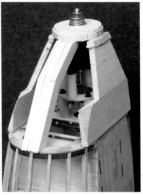
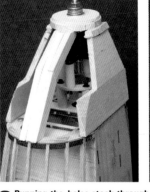

3 Running the balsa stock through a balsa stripper produces pieces of uniform width. This is not necessary, but it does help to keep the weight and dust down and to maximize material yield. Now start gluing pieces in, fitting them as necessary to rough in the contours. Keep cutting and gluing until you have the entire cowl blocked in. It doesn't have to be pretty; you'll get to that next.

4 Now comes the fun part. I removed the forward plywood ring before shaping, and I traced the plywood plate with a pencil for a shaping guide. Roughly shape the cowl and don't fret about the voids; you will fix them later. I used a Master Airscrew razor plane followed by a 1.5x9-inch flat, coarse Perma-Grit hand file for the initial shaping.

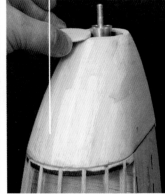

5 Glue more scraps into the voids, and go at it again. A few seconds with the razor plane and Perma-Grit file smoothed these inserts.

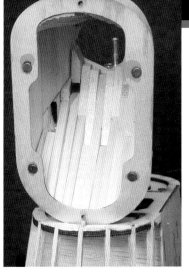

5 Now turn your attention to the inside. I use Robart's Rough 'n' Tough 3/8-inch carbide ball in my Dremel tool to smooth the inner surfaces.

6 Don't worry about a thin spot or two. Repairs are very easy. Just hold the cowl up to a bright light—I used the sky, since I was working outside—and look for thin spots. I poke a hole with a pencil to mark the spot and then press the cowl against my disc sander to create a nice flat area where I attach a filler block.

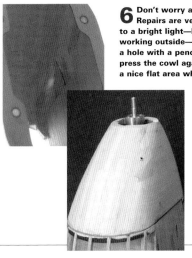

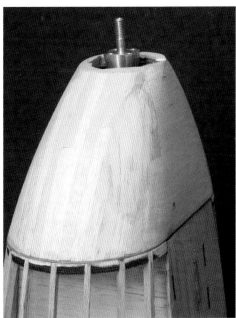

7 This piece is larger than I needed, but it was the first piece I pulled out of the scrap box. A minute or two later, the thin spot has been filled and smoothly faired.

FINISHING UP

At this point, I glued the ply disc to the front of the cowl, opened the hole to clear the prop hub and finished sanding with fine-grit paper. In short order, this cowl was ready for covering!

What about the glue lines? Fresh sandpaper supported by a sanding block will cut right through the CA without raising a ridge. Go lightly with any unsupported sandpaper, or you will leave ridges. The carbide Perma-Grit sanding tools act in the same way and offer the benefit of lasting much longer than conventional sandpaper.

Gather wood and build a cowl. After learning how easy this really is, you will that find many exciting designs are more approachable, and you will have a unique model the next time you go to the field. ✪

Balancing props for smoother flying
Minimize vibration in your models

by Thayer Syme

Vibration is a detrimental force that can result in the premature demise of our models. Even at low energy levels, such persistent forces can cause glue joints to fail and control linkages to wear. Radio components may also be compromised. Not only can the electronic components succumb to vibration, but also wires and connectors can wear to the point of failure.

For maximum enjoyment of our pastime, we need to minimize vibration wherever possible. The two most common sources are the inevitable power pulses from glow and gas engines and propellers that are not perfectly balanced. Since we can't do much about the engine, balancing the propeller is the easiest and most effective way to reduce vibration in your model.

A spinning propeller can vibrate a lot. With typical prop speeds ranging from 2,500rpm in park flyers to 25,000rpm or higher (with more powerful systems), even a slight imbalance can cause vibration. An out-of-balance prop also robs your power system of energy, and I haven't met a modeler yet who was willing to give up power. Fortunately, there are great tools available for fine-tuning the balance of your props.

GETTING STARTED

My balancing techniques depend on the type of prop and the model on which it will be used. Gas and glow engines put higher stresses on the prop and airframe than electric motors do, and wooden props add fuel and moisture protection as additional concerns. While balancing the props, you can also enhance their visibility and safety by painting $1/2$ inch or so of each tip with a bright color such as white or yellow. Since painting the tips can be used for fine-tuning balance, I'll describe it first.

I use a slightly thinned fuelproof paint to paint the tips. To ensure an equal application to each tip, I pour about $1/2$ inch of paint into a yogurt cup. Then I dip a blade into the paint until it touches the bottom of the cup. I let this dry with the wet tip hanging down and then repeat with the second tip. Before I add a second coat, I recheck the balance. If one of the tips is light, I adjust the balance with the amount of paint in the second coat.

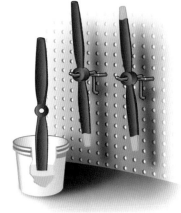

Working on several props at once makes sense, since you can work down your line as the paint dries.

The easiest propellers to balance are the molded plastic and composite props. I start with a single-edge razor blade, carefully scraping off any molding flash. This serves two purposes: smoothing an often

TOOLS

There are a variety of available prop balancers, including Du-Bro's Tru-Spin Prop Balancer, Master Airscrew's Drill Guide Balance System and Top Flite's Magnetic Balancer. These are sophisticated devices with nearly frictionless bearings, and achieving very accurate results is possible. There are also smaller handheld balancers, e.g., the Great Planes Fingertip Prop Balancer that are well-suited to quick checks at the flying field.

While you can check a prop anywhere, I balance my props at home with all my tools and accessories well organized. Beyond a balancer, I find the following items useful.

- Single-edge razor blades
- Clear, strong packing tape
- Clear, fuelproof dope or polyurethane varnish
- Fuelproof white or yellow paint
- Dremel tool with fine sanding drum
- Fine sandpaper
- Paper towels or cotton flannel rags

Once you understand the basics of propeller balancing, getting the job done is pretty simple. With the prop mounted on the balancer, we aim to correct any tendency for the propeller to rotate to a predetermined position. If one blade is heavier than the other, the prop will rotate so that the heavy blade is always lower when the prop stops spinning. A perfectly balanced propeller can be spun slowly and will come to rest in a different position every time. That is what we are trying to achieve.

dangerously sharp leading edge and cleaning up the aerodynamic profile of the blades.

Once I have the flashing smoothed away, I mount the prop on the balancer and check for any imbalance. While these props are usually pretty good right out of the box, rarely are the blades perfectly balanced. Here is where we get into a little bit of the "feel" of balancing. If one blade drops slowly, I know that the blades are close in weight. A slight imbalance can probably be corrected by continuing to scrape the heavy blade with the razor. Don't try to correct a large imbalance by scraping, though. You are inevitably changing the airfoil, and by removing material, you are reducing the ultimate strength of the prop. After balancing a prop or two, you should have developed a feel for how much correction the scraping can offer without compromising durability. Be very careful not to leave any sharp scratches. These will become stress risers and will create a fatigue point that will cause a prop to throw a blade with a high-powered motor.

Instead of scraping, a safer and often easier technique to adjust balance is to add weight to the lighter blade. An extra coat or two of paint on one tip will often do the job. For electric models, tape is also an effective option that is quick and easy to apply and adjust. While traditional desk tapes will work, I also like to use a heavier, high-quality plastic packing tape or even electrical tape. Apply a thin strip to the back of the blade. Trim the tape carefully at the leading and trailing edges with the razor, and recheck the balance. Lightly rest the tape on the prop until you know you have the right size piece and that it is positioned on the blade properly. Once I am happy with the final trim, I burnish the tape down with a fingernail. Tape should not be used for props on glow models since it is not fuel-proof. An extra coat or two of paint on the tips should suffice for these props.

Wooden props must be treated a little differently. Since they don't have molding flash, you can start by checking the initial balance and fine-tuning it as necessary by painting the tips or adding tape. Larger imbalances can be addressed by lightly sanding the blades with fine sandpaper and resealing them with two or three coats of fuel-proof dope. More coats can be added to either side as necessary. I use a piece of paper towel or a scrap of flannel cloth to wipe the dope on, as this seems to apply a smoother and thinner coat than using a brush.

Once you have the prop balanced from side to side, you might notice that it still doesn't stop randomly but comes to rest with a particular blade always to one side. This may mean that the hub itself is out of balance. Since the stresses at the hub can be quite high, I don't like to remove much

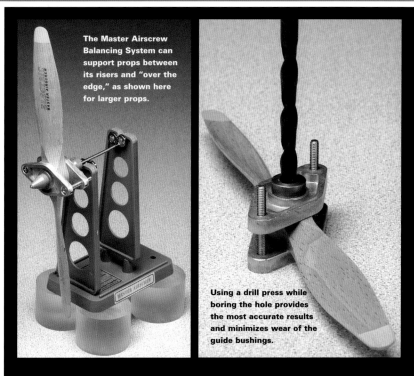

The Master Airscrew Balancing System can support props between its risers and "over the edge," as shown here for larger props.

Using a drill press while boring the hole provides the most accurate results and minimizes wear of the guide bushings.

MASTER AIRSCREW

The Master Airscrew Drill Guide Balance System takes a different approach to balancing props. Instead of sanding, taping, or painting, the Drill Guide system allows you to make subtle adjustments to the location of the hole to balance the prop. The prop is held in a clamp that then guides an included drill bit to enlarge and reposition the hole. This balances the prop with respect to the blades and the hub. Guide bushings are available for $5/16$- and $3/8$-inch holes. This is a unique approach, and it's one that works well for any application that uses holes of these sizes.

In use, I found that adjusting the prop in the clamp was quite easy to do, and it usually only took a few moments to achieve an acceptable balance. The special flat-tip drill bit cleanly bores the hole in the hub at its new location. With the props I balanced to write this article, the enlarged hole encompassed the previous existing hole. None ended up as oblong holes that might have proved confusing when mounting the prop. I found that it was easiest to paint the tips first as desired and then balance and bore the new hole after the paint had cured. This accommodates any variance in the paint as part of the balancing process.

Master Airscrew recommends the use of a drill press while boring the new hole. I found that while a drill press is definitely preferred for accuracy and safety, you can also use a hand drill if you work slowly and carefully.

If you find you are reaming your props to $5/16$ or $3/8$ holes with any regularity, this balancing system is a great option to consider.

material here. I limit myself to smoothing the corners on a wooden prop with a Dremel tool and fine sanding drum, and then I reseal the wood with dope or urethane varnish. You can also build up weight on a hub by sanding lightly to remove the gloss and then applying a few coats of dope, varnish or even epoxy.

A strip of electrical tape quickly balanced this prop for electric models.

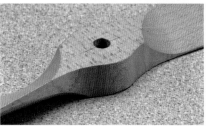

The Great Planes Fingertip Prop Balancer is great for quick checks at the field, and the threaded shaft really lets you lock the prop in place.

The unthreaded ends of the Fingertip Balancer shaft are a perfect fit in the hubs of GWS slow flyer props. The Top Flite Magnetic Balancer will hold this shorter shaft and make balancing these props a snap.

When the dope has cured, you can lightly re-sand these coatings to balance the hub. Master Airscrew composite props have hollow compartments in the hub. These are a great aid to balancing. Bits of modeling clay can be inserted as balancing weights.

If a new prop is way out of balance, I will not take extraordinary measures to fix it. Occasional manufacturing variances or differences in wood density can render a prop too far out of balance to make it safe. Saving a few dollars is simply not worth it when it comes to the risks associated with flying with a prop that might not be sound.

Fingertip prop balancers are great for the field box. If you break your last 11x6 at the field, you might find a buddy who's willing to loan you one. Having a balancer will allow you to make a quick check of the new prop. Though I don't recommend using tape on a glow-powered prop, I would in this case. A small strip of electrical tape out near the tip can do wonders to smooth out a prop for the day. Make sure the prop is completely clean before you apply the tape, and use fuelproof techniques to finish the job properly back at the

Smoothing the corners as shown above will help to balance a heavy hub on a wooden prop. Be sure to reseal the sanded areas before you use the prop. Hollow areas in the Master Airscrew hubs will accept balance weights of glue or clay.

workshop. While you are at it, be sure to balance a replacement prop for your friend!

CONCLUSION

Balancing propellers is easy once you have a few basic tools. You can balance a number of propellers in a single evening and make them safer at the same time. Your models will reward you with a longer life, since they will no longer be shaken to the bones while you fly. You may also find that your models are quieter, as the drumming of the covering material will be greatly reduced or even eliminated. Add a few percentage points of potential power increase, and the benefits of balancing should be clear to all. ✪

Left: Du-Bro's Tru-Spin Prop Balancer has locking cones that securely center propellers of any size on the balancing shaft. Right: Top Flite's Magnetic Balancer has nearly frictionless bearings and is easy to store in its risers.

Drilling large holes in thin balsa wood

by Jerry Nelson

Balsa can be a difficult wood to drill smooth holes in, especially holes of over $5/16$ inch diameter. There is more to it than just having a sharp drill. Here is an easy way to make larger holes.

By using hardware-store spade drills, you can easily make holes of up to $1^1/2$-inch diameters in thin balsa, and between $1/8$- and $1/4$-inch diameters in light-ply and birch plywood. Spade drills are often used to make large holes in 2x4s for wiring and plumbing projects in home construction. What is unique about these drills is that they have a very sharp point on their end. These points act like a milling machine fly-cutter. When you cut a hole, only the outside edge of the spade drill does the cutting. A regular drill removes all of the material when forming the hole.

The center point of the spade drill allows you to place the drill exactly where you want the hole. When you drill wood, a small center hole or starter hole is not required. A drill press is required to drill the hole when you use spade drills. It is important that the wood is perpendicular to the drill so that the ends of the drill cut evenly. When cutting thin wood, the drill should be run at a high-speed setting. A wooden

block must be used as a base. The base allows the guide, or center drill portion of the spade drill, to support itself and prevents the drill from moving. It is important to place the wood you are cutting on a smooth, non-drilled piece of wood, which acts as a base. Scrap plywood or particle board works well. The wooden base supports the cutting forces of the spade drill.

You can also use the spade drill to make large holes in thin aluminum. When you drill aluminum, run the drill press at a low speed. I also recommend that you clamp the part to be drilled to a stable fixture.

Lightening holes can reduce the weight of lightweight RC models such as indoor and park flyers. Each lightening hole alone may not reduce weight much, but when you add the weight saved by drilling several holes, it can be as much as a couple of ounces. This is significant, especially with respect to smaller models. Many of the smaller models are covered with a transparent film, so the outlines of

Drilling requires a drill press and a wooden block under the wood being drilled. Here, I'm drilling a $1^1/2$-inch-diameter hole in the $1/16$-inch SIG balsa. The hole on the right was made with a spade drill bit.

Lightening holes in an $1/8$-inch sheet-balsa park flyer rudder. Weight saved: 0.18 ounce.

the lightening holes are very visible.

It is difficult to make good-looking round holes with a knife. The spade drill does a professional job. Spade drill bits are available at home building and hardware stores. Be certain to get the kind with the sharp tips on the end. ☻

Spade drills can be used to make large holes in thin wood or aluminum. Sizes available are $3/8$ inch to $1^1/2$ inches; the shank diameter is $1/4$ inch. The sharp tip on the end of the drill bit forms an excellent smooth edge in balsa.

3 RADIO SYSTEM & LINKAGE SETUPS

Our RC aircraft are, at their core, high-technology engineering marvels, with control systems that would have amazed modelers only a few short years ago. But to get the most out of our computerized, programmable radio systems, basic setup techniques need to be employed. Many setup secrets from master modelers are included in this chapter. Eye-opening articles on control horns and pushrods include important techniques for optimal linkage installation.

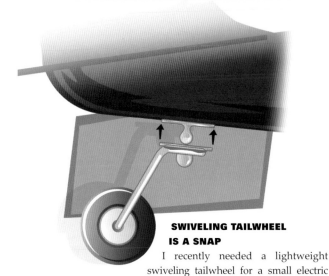

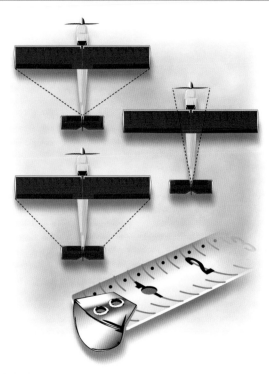

SWIVELING TAILWHEEL IS A SNAP

I recently needed a lightweight swiveling tailwheel for a small electric P-51, and I found that what I needed was a standard clothing snap. The snaps are strong, they swivel easily and cost only pennies. They can also be used to hold hatch covers and canopies in place and perhaps even the wing on smaller models. The snaps come in various sizes and can easily be soldered or epoxied into place. I glued the male side to the bottom of the fuselage and soldered the tailwheel wire to the mating side. I haven't had trouble with the pieces separating on the ground.

SIMPLE AIRFRAME ALIGNMENT

When aligning a new model, accurately measuring the flying surface-to-fuselage distances can be challenging. Here is a method I have used for years to set up my airplanes. Drill an $1/8$-inch hole near the end of your tape measure, and pin it to the top of the fin or the tail to align the wing. Check the stabilizer by pinning the tape measure to the model's nose. You can also confirm the proper thrust alignment for the engine by checking the prop tips. You will find this a lot easier than stretching a string and hoping that you are pulling equally on each end.

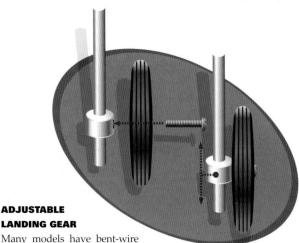

ADJUSTABLE LANDING GEAR

Many models have bent-wire landing gear, and kits often have a straight piece of wire that you have to bend to shape. Once we've bent the wire, the axle height is fixed and the alignment is very difficult to alter. Like many modelers, I have made mistakes that resulted in the wheels' aiming in different directions and being at different heights. I came up with a simple solution that's light, easy to install and, best of all, easy to adjust. Instead of bending the wire to form the axle, slide a wheel collar on and replace the setscrew with a longer, steel, machine screw that can act as the axle. The screw head makes a neater wheel retainer than an external wheel collar, and you can loosen it at any time to adjust toe-in and axle height. Once you've found a setting that works well for you, tighten the screw enough to lightly mark the wire strut, and then grind a small flat on the strut with your Dremel tool for the screw to seat against. A little Loctite will hold the parts together and prevent the assembly from sliding.

EASY ALIGNMENT FOR MOUNTING FINS

I often read about using triangles or squares to align the fin while you glue it into place. But I've never read how to get around the contours of the fuselage or prevent glue from being squeezed out. I glued pieces of spruce on the vertical faces of two lightweight plastic speed squares. The wide bases let them stand upright on the horizontal stab, and the spruce standoffs let you hold the fin without bumping into the fuselage or gluing the squares into place.

SECURE ANTENNA EXIT

CA a small length of fuel tubing through a hole in the fuselage and pass the antenna through it on the way up to the tip of the fin. I make the hole slightly small for a snug fit. This will relieve shock loads just like the tip on a fishing pole.

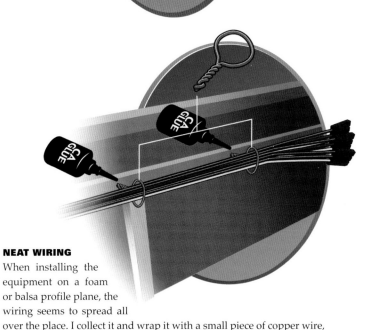

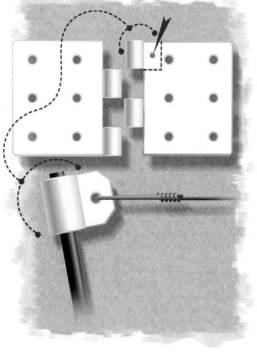

NEAT WIRING

When installing the equipment on a foam or balsa profile plane, the wiring seems to spread all over the place. I collect it and wrap it with a small piece of copper wire, twisted a few times to lock it together. I then cut off about $1/4$ inch of the twisted end and push this end into the fuse before securing it with a drop of CA.

PARK FLYER PULL-PULL CONTROL HORN

I recently completed an IFO MK3 and wish to share with you the changes that I made in the installation of the control horns for a pull-pull setup. The Du-Bro $1/4$-scale heavy-duty hinges fit perfectly on the .050-inch solid carbon rod. A small hole was drilled in the stock hinge prior to cutting out the horn pieces. After cutting the carbon rod to the desired length, each end was fitted with one of these newly made pieces and the assembly was then mounted to the control surface to complete the installation. Works well for me and the price is right!

ANTENNA MANAGEMENT

This technique will clean up your small flat foam park flyer antennas with minimal distance loss in your radio reception. Run your antenna wire about 5 to 6 inches down the fuselage side, then use a T-pin slightly larger than the diameter of your antenna to poke about 25 to 35 holes evenly spaced about $1/4$ inch apart and $1/4$ inch from the bottom of the fuselage. Gently thread the antenna through the holes like shoe laces all the way down the fuselage. Make sure you do not overlap the antenna on itself, and leave a little slack in the laces for movement while the plane is flexing in flight. Once you get to the rear of the fuselage, route the antenna up the rudder or down the horizontal stabilizer, leaving about 6 to 8 inches of straight antenna after the laces. Range-check your model with the motor on and off before flying.

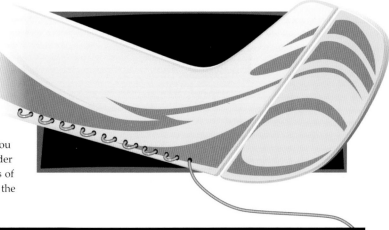

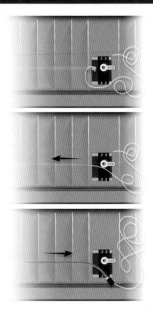

PROTECTIVE FOAM

A kneeling pad is a great source of foam for protecting your receiver, batteries and fuel tank from impact and vibration. It's easy to cut and weighs very little. Just be sure that the kneeling pad you cut up is yours!

REPLACING
EXTENSION-LEAD PULLS

Now you've done it! You have a beautiful ARF, but you've pulled out the string that the manufacturer included for pulling the servo leads through. Now what? I found two easy ways to solve this one: get a piece of music wire long enough to reach the cutout for the servo, push it through the holes provided, and then tie a piece of string to the servo lead and the wire and pull it through. Alternatively, use a piece of $^1/4$ square balsa with a slit cut in one end. Push that end from the wing root to the servo cutout. Then take a string or a length of fishing line and tie a knot in one end. Slide the string into the slit you cut, pull it taut until the knot is against the wood, and then slowly pull the stick back out along with the string you just attached.

EASY SETUP
PULL-PULL CONTROLS

While building my Mini 3DX foamie, I came up with a simple, light pull-pull system that eliminates the need to get the cables just so. I used 0.015 music wire instead of cables or thread. It is lighter than the usual carbon-fiber setup and much more positive. Put Z-bends at every end. One pull wire has only Z-bends; the other also has a jog in it to adjust the tension. It's such fine wire that it is relatively easy to get a precise length even with the Z-bend. Hardly any tension is required for a slop-free, tight linkage.

DIY TRANSMITTER STAND

If you want to stand your transmitter upright while you start your engine, make a foldable stand out of music wire. All you need is music wire of any diameter and four wire straps. Bend the music wire as shown in the picture, slide it into place, and cross-strap it into the transmitter handle. This stand will cost you next to nothing.

UNPLUG SERVOS THE EASY WAY

Removing tight servo plugs from a small receiver can be awkward, especially if you have large fingers. I tie small loops of thread around my servo plugs. These finger loops make it a lot easier to unplug the servos without tugging on the wires.

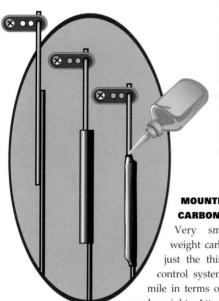

MOUNTING PARK FLYER CARBON-FIBER CONTROLS

Very small-diameter, light-weight carbon-fiber rods can be just the thing for home-brewed control systems that go the extra mile in terms of eliminating slop and weight. Attach a 0.040-inch diameter section of music wire with a Z-bend to a 0.036-inch-diameter carbon-fiber control rod with the narrow heat-shrink tubing that you would usually use when you solder servo leads, and then wick in thin CA. Be sure to anchor the control rod with pushrod shrouds every few inches to minimize play in the system.

LIGHTWEIGHT SWITCHES

I use dress snaps as lightweight switches. Solder a wire to the rim of each half, and you only have to press the two parts together to get a problem-free connection. You can attach one side to the model or let both sides swing free. The sewing area in any department store carries these in a number of sizes.

"BLIND" TRANSMITTER KNOB

I like to use flaperons or spoilers on my models, but I don't like to look away from my plane while I'm flying to see whether I have the correct knob or to check its position. My transmitter has a dial for channel 6, and it is difficult to know where it is set without looking. To solve this dilemma, I installed a 2-56 socket-head capscrew on the top of the knob. I removed the knob from the transmitter with a hex wrench, and I drilled a no. 51-drill-bit hole in the knob and threaded it with a 2-56 tap. The screw provides instant tactile feedback that allows me to easily adjust the control without looking.

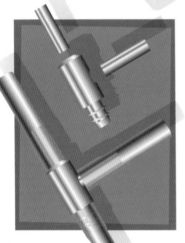

ELIMINATE FOAM-PADDING HANGUPS

After you've wrapped components such as tanks, receivers and battery packs in protective foam rubber, fitting them into tight spots can be difficult. The foam tends to catch on structures such as bulkheads. Wrap the item and foam with Glad Press'n Seal. The wrap holds tight; it can shape or taper the foam, and it slides easily over or through bare wood surfaces. You can even leave one end longer and form it into a pull tab to make removing the components easy.

PET FLEX TO THE RESCUE

Pet Flex—a flexible adhesive wrap that you can buy at most pet stores— has many uses in the RC shop. I use wrap of various colors to mark the servo-lead pairs between the fuselage and the wing for the ailerons and flaps. When I disconnect them, the colored wrap makes it easy to reconnect them correctly. Pet Flex also provided a great save when I forgot to slide a small piece of fuel tubing onto the pushrod to secure a tight, aileron-linkage nylon snap-link.My many attempts to slide the tubing over the snap link failed, and the plane's narrow confines made it incredibly difficult to unscrew it. I cut a narrow piece of Pet Flex and wrapped it tightly around the snap-link.

SIMPLE MECHANICAL SERVO MOUNT

Mold-release residue on the inside of molded fiberglass or composite fuselages can prevent balsa servo-mounting rails from staying glued inside.This tip solves the problem, saves a little weight and removes clutter. Take the four tiny mounting screws out of the bottom of the servo case and remove the case from the servo. The case serves as a template for drilling mounting holes through the fuse. After drilling the first hole, drop a mounting screw through the case hole and let it anchor the case while you drill the next hole; then drop that screw through. You can also drill the holes externally with the case pressed against the outside of the fuse; that works just as well.

SIMPLE MECHANICAL SERVO MOUNT

Mold release residue on the inside of molded glass or composite fuselages can prevent balsa servo mounting rails from staying glued to the fuselage interior. This technique solves the problem, saves a tiny amount of weight and removes clutter. Take the four tiny mounting screws out of the bottom of the servo case and remove the case from the servo. The case serves as a template for drilling mounting holes through the fuse. After drilling the first hole, drop a mounting screw through the case hole and let it anchor the case while you drill the next hole, then drop that screw through. You can also drill the holes externally with the case pressed against the outside of the fuse—this works just as well.

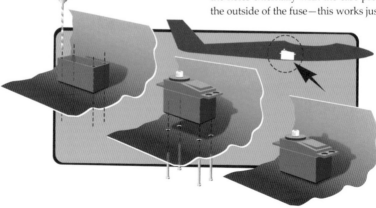

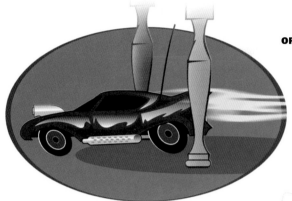

ORIENTATION TRAINING

Are you just starting to fly RC airplanes? I advise all newcomers to buy a cheap RC car and drive it around while the glue is drying on their airplanes. Tie a ribbon at the rear and try to keep it free of the cat's claws as you race it around under the kitchen table. All this practice will get you used to moving the transmitter stick in the correct direction when the vehicle is coming back to you, and it helps you to avoid crashing your new plane. Of course, PC flight sims offer the same capability, and a lot more, but this is cheaper and a lot of fun—for you and your cat!

PERSONALIZED FREQUENCY CARDS

I take a photo of each new project and enclose it in a self-sealing lamination pouch with my name, the model name, its channel number and the date it first flew.. I then leave this on our club frequency board so that anyone looking for a pin will know not only who has it but also what the model looks like.

Jim Miller
Ch. #31
Trainer 40
July 06

UNTANGLE SERVO LEADS

I recently built a Hangar 9 AT6 and incorporated flaperons. With all the wires I had to hook up when I put the wing on, I came up with this idea to keep everything neat. I cut three slots to tightly fit the servo-extension connectors in a piece of $3/8$-inch-square balsa, and I glued on another piece of $3/8$ square balsa in front of them. I glued this assembly to the wing to hold the mounting plates in the fuselage. It makes it easy to hook up the leads, and it also looks neat.

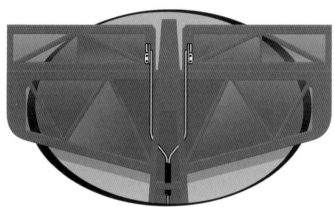

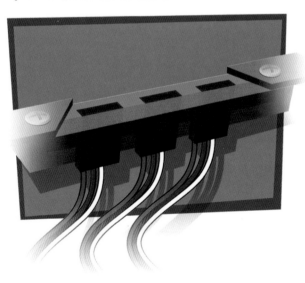

STRONGER SPLIT ELEVATOR CONTROL

If you have an ARF with split elevators and you want a stronger elevator control setup than the traditional torque-rod and control-horn, make a Y in the control rod as shown. Bend music wire to the needed shape, wrap the ends of the two arms with uncoated copper wire to bind them to the control rod that extends to the servo, and solder-fill the wrapped joint.

EMERGENCY SERVO SCREWS

I dropped the little servo-arm screw and didn't have any spares. What to do? I found an exact replacement in an old pair of sunglasses. You could salvage a screw as I did or buy a reading-glasses repair kit at the supermarket.

LIGHT TIMER CHARGING

Charging transmitter and receiver batteries means watching the clock to make sure that charging times are long enough. Use a light timer to start and stop the charging time, and you can get up early in the morning and be ready for a day of flying.

EASY ANTENNA MOUNT

RadioShack heat-shrink tubing has a glossy surface and can serve as a handy antenna support. Simply mount the tubing (no heat-shrinking involved) in the fuselage and slide the antenna through it. This relieves the antenna, as there is no sharp bend where it exits the fuse, and it looks good as well.

TRANSMITTER CARRIER

I use a cheap "carabineer" clipped to my transmitter handle to attach the transmitter to my belt when I pick my park flyer up. This keeps the transmitter secure and allows me to disconnect the battery with both hands. I bought mine at an office supply store.

WIRING FIRST AID

When I need to insulate wiring connections at the field and don't have any electrical tape handy, instead of not flying, I use a medium or large Band-Aid from my first-aid kit. I cut out the gauze pad and have two pieces of very flexible sticky tape that can be used to wrap an exposed electrical joint. I have used this material for many years with great success.

CLEAN SERVO MOUNTING

If you're just just getting into electrics, you'll be interested in this servo-mounting method. It's great when screws are not suitable and I want a more secure bond than servo tape provides. Gluing servos into place is not the answer because you have to scrape the glue off when you reuse them for another plane, and glue can get into the servo cases. When assembling a new LiPo pack, I used heat-shrink tubing to hold two packs together and I had an idea: I used heat-shrink tubing to sleeve the servos and glued them in with a little Shoe-Goo. No more glued cases or crud to clean off the sides of the servos. This can also work with other components.

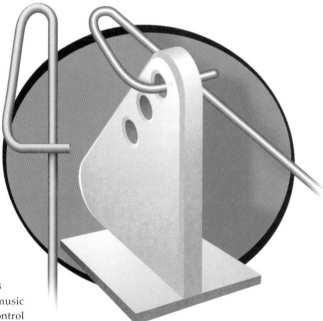

MAGNETIC SALVATION

I hope that the following tip can be of some help to my fellow modelers. I had to replace a servo gear set at a recent contest. When I put the servo case back together, I noticed that a case screw had fallen off my flight box and into the grass. After 15 minutes of frustration, I waved my Top Flite Precision Magnetic prop balancer over the area of the lost screw; the screw jumped from the grass to the magnet and I was back in the air in minutes!

EASY RELEASE CONTROL-ROD BENDS

The typical Z-bent music wire that connects control rods to control horns has to be inserted into the control-horn hole at an angle that requires the removal of the other end of the control rod from the servo. This wrap-around bend is much easier to attach and remove: just pull the wire out of the control-horn hole, and the control rod is free and doesn't have to be rotated at an angle or detached from the servo horn.

Control-Horn Basics
Mechanics made easy

by Jason Carter

This was written in response to a letter from a reader of *Fly RC*:

What's the best way to install the aileron, rudder, or elevator control horns that come with most kits? I have been building for over 30 years, and this remains my least favorite part of the build. The screws always seem to be just a little off when I try to put them through the aileron to fasten the horn to the plastic attachment on the other side.

When this arrived, I was building a J-3 Cub with floats. The only frustrating part of the entire build was installing the control horns so that the screws passed through the aileron control surfaces and into the keeper plates as they should. I took comfort from hearing that a 30-year-veteran of the hobby shared my frustration.

WHAT OTHERS SAY

We bounced the topic around the *Fly RC* office to find the best solution—one that would work well and serve as a universal guide to installing control horns. We realized that because control surfaces differ, creating a jig for drilling the holes wouldn't be a solution. This is because the control horns are typically installed after the control surfaces have been hinged and installed. To further complicate things, some modelers say that they don't worry if they don't get the holes through control surfaces absolutely perfect. Some say that they do try to get the holes perfect by drilling through the control surface while keeping the bit as perpendicular to the surface as they can. One modeler even suggests drilling the hole slightly oversize and epoxying a short section of brass tube into the control surface to strengthen the structure. Several others say that they work the screws into place if they are slightly off and then apply CA to the underlying wood to strengthen the rim around the screw holes.

TIPS & TRICKS

The best advice I can give is that you should position each control horn and mark every screw hole's position with a fine-point permanent marker. For small aircraft such as park flyers, use a pin vise to drill a small hole through the control surface. On .46 to .60

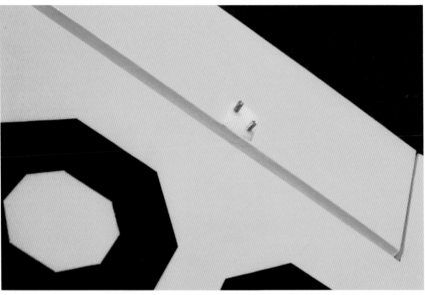

A Du-Bro EZ-link connector is used at the servo side of this 2-56 control linkage while a Du-Bro Qwik-Link is used at the control horn. Notice that the control rod fits very tightly through the servo arm. Remember that slop is your enemy.

To avoid building differential into your control linkages, install your control horn so that the pivot point, where the clevis is attached to your control horn, is directly over your hinge line.

Always trim off the excess length of the exposed screw shanks. It cleans up the model's overall appearance and makes post-flight cleaning less of a hassle.

aircraft, you may get away with using a Dremel tool to drill the screw holes. On larger aircraft that use one pass-through bolt, a cordless drill should work fine.

To avoid building differential into your controls, install the control horns so that the pivot point is over the hinge line. "Differential" is a word used to describe when control-surface throw is greater in one direction than in the other. There are times when you want this, but that's a subject for another time.

Having installed the control horn, trim off the excess screw shank with a set of side cutters or a Dremel tool.

Control-surface slop is your enemy. to eliminate it, use the outer holes in the control horn whenever you can. When you use a control-horn hole that's farther from the hinge point, it takes more servo travel to

DU-BRO CONTROL HORNS

These standard control horns are a subset of those available from Du-Bro, and they indicate the broad range of available sizes and styles.

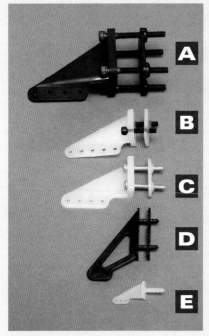

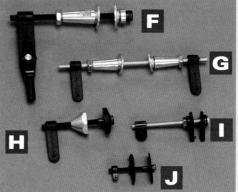

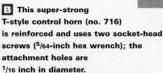

A The Du-Bro large-scale T-style control horn (item no. 366) features 4 socket-head screws (3/32-inch hex wrench) that are bolted through a square baseplate. It's made of tough, reinforced plastic, and the top of the horn extends about 1.4 inches above the control surface. The clevis attachment holes are 1/16 inch in diameter.

B This super-strong T-style control horn (no. 716) is reinforced and uses two socket-head screws (5/64-inch hex wrench); the attachment holes are 1/16 inch in diameter.

C Du-Bro also makes right-handed and left-handed horns with baseplates that extend in one direction or the other. This standard nylon control horn (no. 105) uses pan-head steel screws. Its body is not as thick as those of the heavy-duty horns shown above it.

Du-Bro offers a broad assortment of well-designed, adjustable control horns; some have floating baseplates that seat in a swivel to fit a flat or tapered control surface.

F The Heavy Duty (HD) adjustable horn (no. 913) is designed for .91 glow airplanes and larger. The mounting bolt is 2.9 inches long and can be trimmed to fit. It's a socket-head capscrew (9/64-inch hex wrench). The horn arm is 1.5 inches long and can be trimmed shorter and then redrilled. It has an 1/8-inch-diameter clevis attachment hole and comes with a no-slop clevis that's attached by an aluminum pin that's secured by a miniature cotter pin. The clevis is self-threading and accepts a 4-40 threaded control rod. The top and bottom mounting plates seat in bowl-shaped swivels that allow the plates to conform exactly to the flat or angular cross-sectional shape of the control surface.

D The Micro Razor control horn (no. 936) is very light and streamlined. It's attached with glue not bolts. The attachment plates have cleats on their inner surface to grip the control surface better. The attachment holes are 1/32 inch in diameter.

E The micro control horn (no. 848) is ideal for park flyers and smaller models. There isn't a baseplate; the horn is simply glued into a hole drilled in the control surface. The attachment holes are 1/32 inch in diameter.

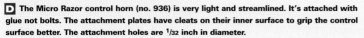

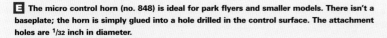

G The HD dual control horn (no. 880) is intended for .40 to .91 aircraft. A larger version exists for .91 and larger airplanes. It has swivel mounting plates that follow the taper of the control surface for a precise fit, and it's perfect for pull-pull rudder applications, etc.

H The HD control horn (no. 867) is intended for .40 to .91 aircraft. It has a 6-32x1/2-inch socket-head capscrew, and the horn arm has a 1/16-inch attachment hole for mounting the clevis. The horn arm can be shortened and redrilled if you want.

I The standard adjustable control horn (no. 493) uses a 5-40 pan-head screw, and the horn arm is self-threading so that you can adjust its height. It has a 1/16-inch clevis attachment hole. The mounting plates have cleats.

J The adjustable micro control horn (no. 935) is ideal for park flyers and smaller aircraft of all types. It has a 1/32-inch clevis attachment hole and is glued to the control surface with foam-safe CA or epoxy. The attachment plates are semicircular and have gripping cleats. A 5/64-inch hex wrench is used to tighten the socket-head mounting capscrew into the self-threading horn arm.

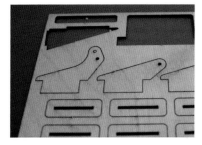

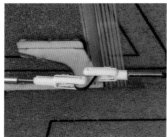

Light-ply is often used for control horns on foamies, and it's easy to make your own if you're scratch-building or making a repair. The laser-cut horns used in the Ikarus S400 Sukhoi have a slotted base through which the horn protrudes into the foam.

achieve the same degree of control-surface deflection than it would if you used a hole in the control horn near its base. You also get more leverage.

Though most models don't present much of a hassle, keep these basics in mind when you install control-surface horns. There are times when modelers must get creative with control-surface linkages and installations. ✪

Heavy-Duty Pushrods & Pushrod Ends

by Jerry Nelson

Pushrods are commonly used for elevator and rudder control systems. Pushrods are also used when ailerons and flaps are driven by bellcranks. Several types of pushrod material can be utilized. Here, I discuss the most commonly used pushrod materials found in the larger scale and aerobatic type models. Often overlooked is an explanation of ways to attach a device securely to the pushrod end that will allow a clevis fitting to be attached to a control horn, a bellcrank, or a servo arm. We will now look at four methods of attachments and four different types of pushrod materials.

ATTACHMENTS

Pushrods should be supported in the middle, especially those that are longer than 24 inches or so. There are two reasons for this. When the pushrod is pulling on the control surface, there is no problem, but when it's pushing the control surface, the pushrod might bend under the air load created while the model is in flight. The other concern is the effect of G-loads on the pushrod. When the model is doing tight loops or turns, the weight of the pushrod increases in direct proportion to the Gs pulled in the maneuver. This can cause the pushrod to bend, thereby causing the control-surface travel to be different from what is actually desired.

To solve this problem, position a pushrod guide about halfway along the length of the pushrod. This guide must not be a close fit. For example, if a $^3/_{16}$-inch pushrod is used, have a guide with a $^5/_{16}$-inch hole. The hole should be big enough for the pushrod not to bind when the control surfaces are moved to their maximum positions. A piece of $^1/_{16}$-inch plywood is good. A hardwood lollipop or ice cream bar stick will work well, too.

A larger pushrod would take care of any excessive air loads or G-loads, but then the weight of the pushrod becomes an issue, especially if the model is inclined to be tail-heavy. When using a long pushrod, it is much better to use a light one and support it halfway.

Simple, practical pushrod materials for larger models are $^1/_4$ x$^1/_4$-inch spruce or $^1/_4$-inch hardwood dowels. Hard balsa can also be used. It is important to have the pushrod ends attached at the center of the pushrod. If they

A $^1/_4$-inch-diameter dowel or $^1/_4$x$^1/_4$ inch spruce (available from SIG Mfg.) makes satisfactory low-cost pushrods. The method shown is easy and allows the proper centering of the $^1/_{16}$-inch-diameter piano-wire pushrod extension. A soldered brass sleeve attaches $^1/_{16}$- inch-diameter piano wire thrust wire (one with the 90-degree bent end) securely to the wire pushrod extension. The end of the $^1/_{16}$-inch pushrod extension can be fitted with several types of attachments that can be connected to the control arm, bellcrank, or servo arm.

are attached off to one side, the pushrod may bend under load. You cannot simply drill a hole in the end of a wooden pushrod and CA a wire pushrod extension into it. This is not a secure attachment, and it is highly likely that the wire would pull out under high load conditions.

You might also be tempted to drill a hole in the end of the pushrod to accept a 4-40 tap and then simply thread in a 4-40 threaded rod. This is not a good idea, since the strength of threads in end-grain wood is not adequate.

A simple way to attach a $^1/_{16}$-inch -diameter piano-wire pushrod extension to the center of the wooden pushrod is to drill a $^1/_{16}$-inch hole about 1 inch deep. Then bend a $^1/_{16}$-inch-diameter piano-wire thrust wire as shown. Drill a cross-hole through the wooden pushrod. Cut a piece of $^1/_8$-inch-i.d. brass tube about $^1/_2$ inch long. Next, place the $^1/_{16}$-inch piano-wire extension in the wooden pushrod. Insert the 90-degree end of the thrust wire through the pushrod. Now slide the $^5/_{32}$-inch diameter brass tube sleeve over both wires as shown. Solder the brass tube sleeve into place. Note that the 90-degree end of the thrust wire must extend beyond the wooden pushrod by about $^1/_{16}$ to $^3/_{32}$ inch. A no. 2 or similar washer is then soldered to the wire. This keeps the thrust wire securely in place. You could alternatively bind the wire to the pushrod with

Nelson Hobbies offers 6061T-6 hard $^3/_{16}$-inch diameter aluminum tube with a 0.049-inch-thick wall that makes excellent pushrods. Lengths are from 11$^3/_4$ to 35$^3/_4$ inches. Inside diameter is just right for a 4-40 tap. Tap the tube about $^1/_4$ to $^5/_{16}$ inch deep. If you cannot find a 4-40 tap, Du-Bro sells a convenient package of tap drills and taps (DUB361, $23.80) and an individual 4-40 drill and tap set (DUB361, $4.40). Screw in a 4-40x1-inch setscrew or use a 4-40 capscrew or machine screw instead. When the screw has been tightened, cut off the screw head.

Kevlar thread. Glue the thrust wire to the sides of the wooden pushrod and saturate the thread (if used) with Zap-A-Gap CA.

This simple attachment system is designed using easily obtainable materials. It may not be very high-tech, but it *is* practical and it works well.

NELSON HOBBY SPECIALTIES

Aluminum tube pushrods Another pushrod system is made using hard aluminum tubes. Aluminum tube is available in various degrees of hardness. For this application, the tube must be the hardest–T-6 aluminum.

The ideal aluminum tube is $3/16$ inch in diameter 6061T-6 with a 0.049-inch-thick wall. It's light (about 0.4 ounce per foot) and extremely resistant to being bent. The inside diameter of this tubing is just right for the tapping of a 4-40 thread about $1/4$ to $5/16$ inch deep. A 4-40 threaded rod or screw about $3/4$ inch long or more is threaded into the tube. The threaded rod or screw is then tightened firmly into the tube and held in place because of the taper that is formed at the end of the tapped thread. When a machine screw is installed and tightened into place, cut off the head of the screw. File the end of the screw smooth so a standard 4-40 nut will be easy to thread into place.

With the threaded screw in place, you can easily attach a threaded clevis or a ball link. If you use a metal clevis, I suggest that you install a jam nut next to the clevis. This will prevent the pushrod from turning because of the vibration of the engine.

This type of pushrod is excellent for short elevator and aileron pushrods on larger aerobatic aircraft. Typically, 4-40 ball links are used at each end of the pushrod. The diameters of the ball-link shanks are about the same as the aluminum tube, which can be polished or painted to improve its appearance.

DAVE BROWN PRODUCTS

Fiberglass pushrod system Fiberglass tube for pushrods is available from Dave Brown Products. In each package are two 0.293-inch -diameter pushrods (0.250 i.d.) that are 36 inches long. These are high-quality pushrods and not arrowshaft rejects. They are light and extremely strong.

The five pushrod ends are $1/4$ inch in diameter and are molded from nylon. Two

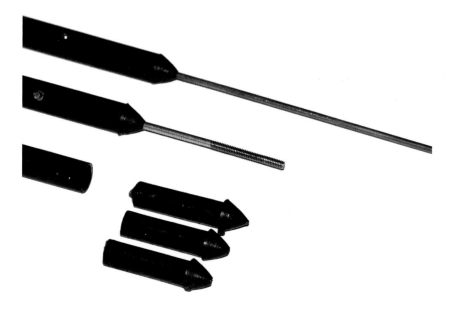

36-inch fiberglass pushrods (2 per pack, $7.95) are available from Dave Brown Products. Diameter is 0.293 inch ($19/64$ inch) and inside diameter is 0.250 inch. Supplied with five nylon fittings. Shown installed is a $1/16$-inch-diameter. wire pushrod and a 2-56 threaded rod. Also available is a unit for two 2-56 threaded rods for a Y setup for split elevators. The end of the $1/16$-inch wire or threaded rod is bent upward by 90 degrees and protrudes out of the pushrod to provide a positive lock.

ends are for use with $1/16$-inch-diameter piano wire; another two are for use with 2-56 clevis rods; and one unit is set up for the installation of two 2-56 clevis rods for split elevators.

The installation is simple. A hole is drilled for the wire or rod about 1 inch from the end of the pushrod. The nylon fitting is placed on the wire or clevis rod. About $1/4$ inch of the clevis rod wire is bent at a 90-degree angle. Slip the bent end into the pushrod and fit it into the previously drilled hole. Put epoxy or CA on the nylon fitting and slipped it into the pushrod. Like the previously described wooden pushrods, the hole that was drilled in the pushrod carries the pushrod extension load. This secure and permanent installation is very easy to make.

CENTRAL HOBBIES

Carbon-fiber pushrods & titanium pushrod ends The strongest and lightest pushrods are made of carbon fiber. Central Hobbies offers carbon fiber pushrods in

four diameters: $1/8$, $5/32$, $3/16$ and $1/4$ inch. Along with the pushrods, Central Hobbies also offers titanium pushrod ends to fit the four sizes of pushrods. Thread sizes are 2-56, 4-40, 6-32, 8-32 and 2, 2.5 and 3mm. Combination pushrod sets are available with two pushrods and four titanium pushrod ends. The pushrod ends are held in place with J-B Weld epoxy, which is also available from Central Hobbies.

In competition, weight is critical, and these are perhaps the lightest units available in the hobby industry.

CONCLUSION

There are several pushrod options for aerobatic and large models on which stresses can be high. The key is to make sure that your pushrods are well supported to prevent them from flexing, they do not bind, and they are stiff enough to withstand the anticipated flight loads. Cover those concerns and you are ready for some great flying! ✪

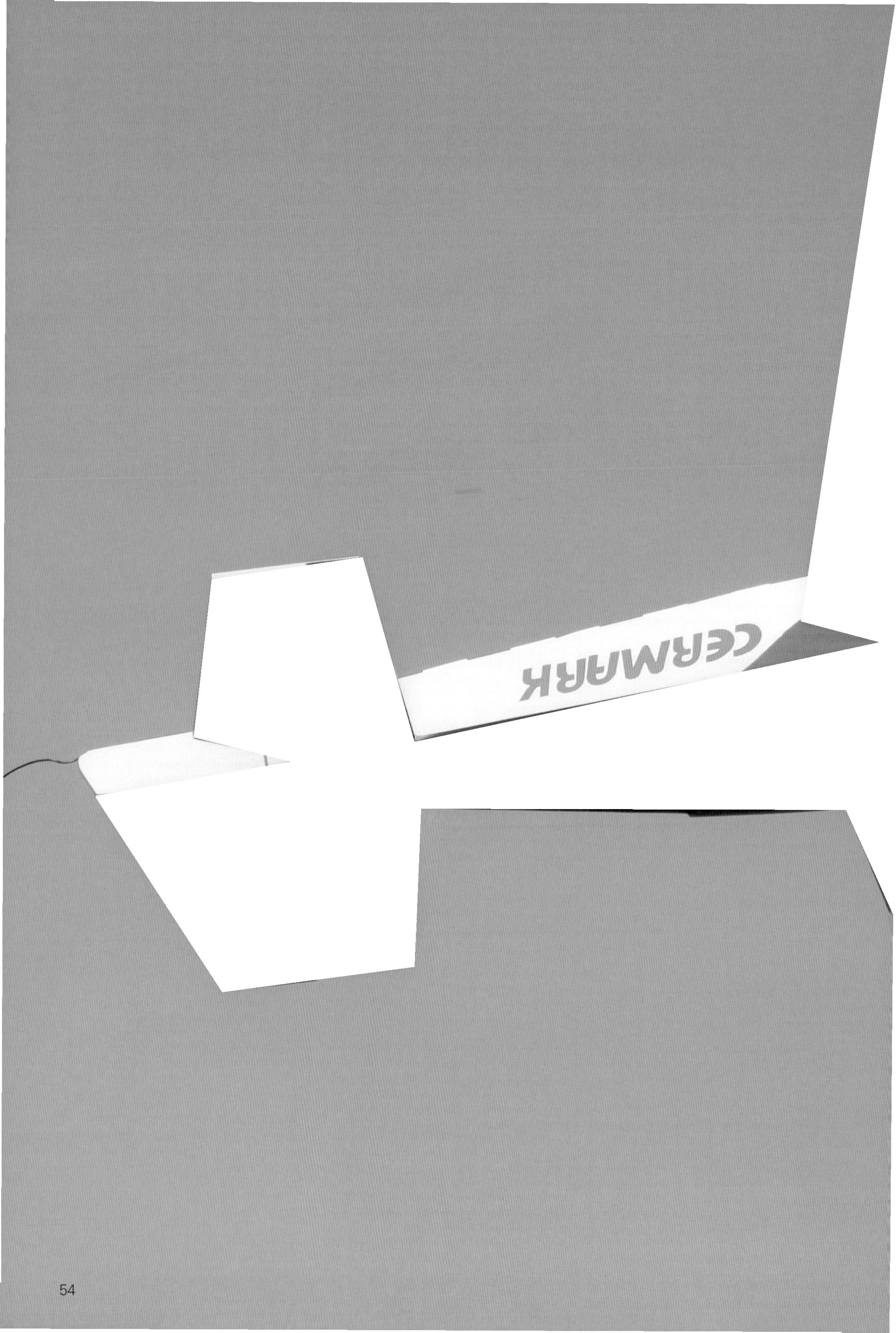
CERMARK

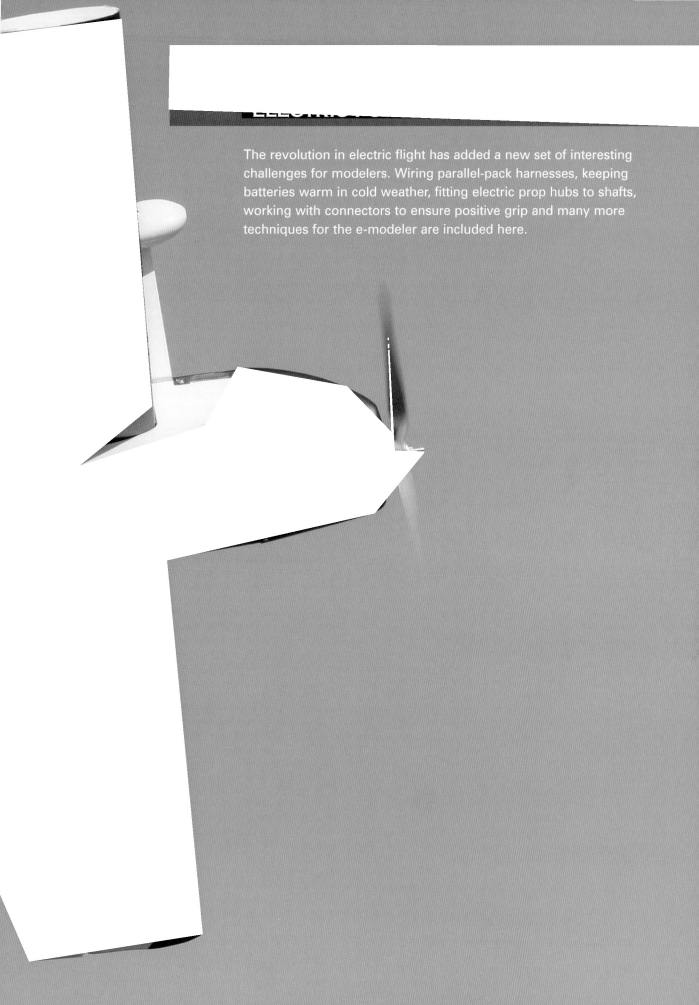

ELECTRICS

The revolution in electric flight has added a new set of interesting challenges for modelers. Wiring parallel-pack harnesses, keeping batteries warm in cold weather, fitting electric prop hubs to shafts, working with connectors to ensure positive grip and many more techniques for the e-modeler are included here.

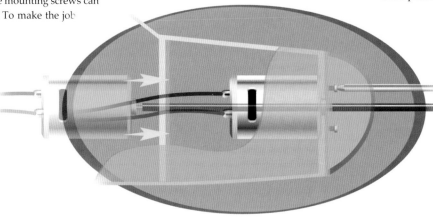

SIMPLE SOLDERING JIG

It's always hard for me to hold wires together precisely while soldering them together, so I made a simple jig out of a Popsicle stick, aluminum foil and two clothespins. Strip the wires and slide the heat-shrink tubing over one wire. Wrap a small piece of foil around the Popsicle stick as insulation, and then use the clothespins to hold the wires against the foil. The insulated stick provides great stability and support as you solder the joint, and the solder won't stick to the foil. Once the joint is secure, you can remove the clips and shrink the tubing to protect the joint. This jig saves me from burning my fingers, keeps the wires straight and makes the solder joint more precise.

FISHING ELECTRIC MOTORS THROUGH FUSELAGES

Electric designs sometimes require that you install the motor through the wing-saddle area. Getting the motor into place and holding it while you install the mounting screws can sometimes require six hands. To make the job easier, press a piece of pushrod tubing onto the motor shaft. You can then use the tubing to fish the motor through the fuselage and hold it in place while you install the motor-mount screws.

CONTROL-ARM MOTOR MOUNT

Looking for a handy way to mount a small brushless motor in a profile 3D park flyer? Modify a servo control arm. Du-Bro Super Strength Servo Arms are made of a sturdy, shock-absorbing material that's strong enough to hold a small motor securely on the frame. One pack will give you a handful of motor mounts. Remove the cylindrical hub that fits over the servo spline, enlarge the arm's center hole if necessary to fit your motor configuration, and bolt the ends of the arms to the fuselage front.

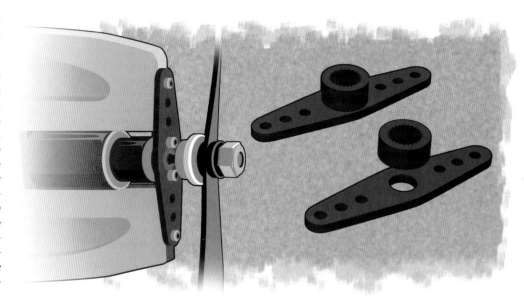

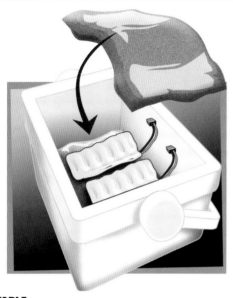

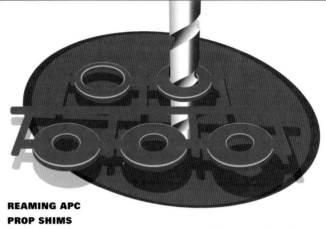

REAMING APC PROP SHIMS

The next time you set up an APC prop, try this. The centering adapter rings often have to be reamed out slightly for a proper fit on the prop shaft. I leave the rings on the molding tree to give myself a good handle while I enlarge the hole. Once it fits over the shaft, you can detach it from the "tree" and mount the prop in the usual way.

PORTABLE BATTERY WARMER

I enjoy flying off snow, and I developed a way to preserve the power in my backup batteries while on the flight line in cold weather. I fill a Ziploc bag with uncooked rice, microwave it for a minute, wrap it around my batteries and put them in a room-temperature insulated cooler. Off to the flight line I go with a supply of charged batteries that will stay at peak power regardless of the cold.

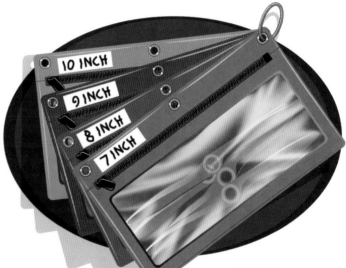

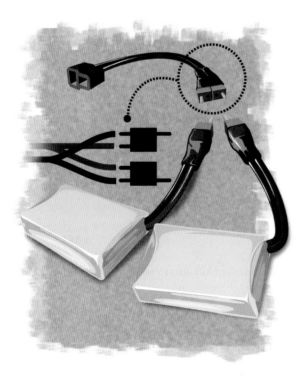

EASY, LIGHT PARALLEL PACK CONNECTOR

Here's a handy, light Y-harness design for connecting LiPo battery packs in parallel to increase the available capacity and discharge rate (for example, 2 1200mAh packs wired in parallel become a single 2400mAh battery with twice the discharge rate of the individual packs). This setup uses four small Deans polarized plugs and a Deans Ultra Plug. Solder the positive and negative leads to the plugs and then shrink-wrap them exactly as shown (red is positive, black is negative).

PROP POUCHES

I fly lots of smaller electrics and have lots of props for my different motors. I always seemed to be searching through all the props in the box to find the right one. Then I came up with this idea: I use pencil pouches from any office supply store to store all the sizes. I joined the pouches with binder rings and marked each pouch with the prop diameter. They will hold props up to 11 inches. Now I can find the right prop quickly and the pouches are cheap. Works great.

KEEP CONNECTORS CLEAN

I use MPI and Jeti electrical connectors, sizes 2.5 and 3.5m
Sometimes, the solder flows onto the outside of the connector or i
the slots on the male connectors. To avoid this when soldering, sli
short piece of $3/32$-inch-i.d. silicone fuel hose over the end of the conr
tor before you start. This will prevent any solder from flowing ou
control and down the connector! Neat, foolproof connections!

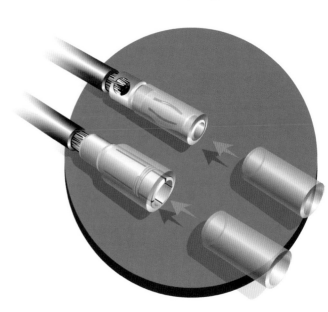

VELCRO MANAGEMENT

Velcro is popular for holding motor batteries on the fuselage tray. It
can be tricky to get the battery back into the fuselage because the
strap ends want to curl back and grab each other. I glue small pieces
of the opposing Velcro material to the fuselage sides to hold the
straps neatly out of the way.

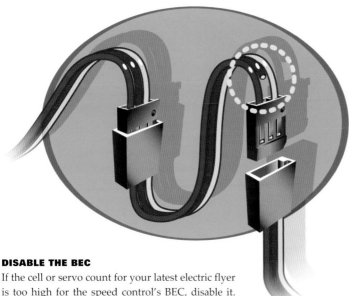

DISABLE THE BEC

If the cell or servo count for your latest electric flyer
is too high for the speed control's BEC, disable it.
Instead of cutting the control's red lead or pulling its
pin out of the plug, I buy a 6-inch servo extension
and modify its red lead. When I need to reactivate
the BEC without a hassle, I just remove this
extension.

INSTANT PROP-SHAFT ADAPTER

Many of us have reamed out prop hubs and then wanted to put
the prop on a shaft that is too skinny to center it. A quick fix for
both glow and electric airplanes is to tightly wind electrical tape
around the prop shaft until it properly centers the prop. Then cut
off the excess length with a single-edge razor blade. The prop nut
will hold the now centered prop tightly against the adapter backplate. Problem solved.

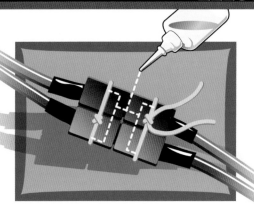

POSITIVE GRIP FOR FIRM CONNECTORS

I don't like to pull on any wires to separate connectors, but some of the high-current connectors such as the large Deans Ultra and the Astro Flight Zero Loss can be very hard to separate because they are so smooth and there is not much to grip with your fingers. Tie a string around the connector body and put a couple of drops of thin CA on the string to bond it to the connector. When the CA has set, clip off the ends of the string. It takes only a minute and provides a positive grip that makes it easy to mate and separate connectors.

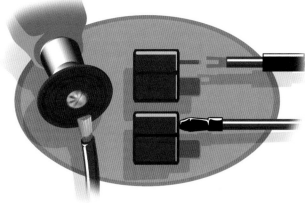

HUB-GRIPPING SURFACE

Since I have changed to brushless motors, I have had trouble with the smooth hub on many prop adapters. I now use an electric engraver to create a pattern of small circles on the hub faces. This makes a rough surface that grips the prop and transfers all the motor power efficiently.

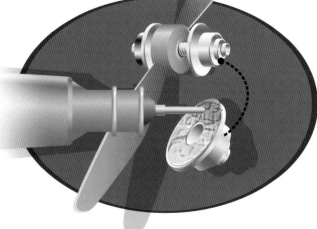

STRONGER SOLDER JOINTS

When you solder large-gauge wire to Deans Ultra connectors, there's a way to make a neater and electrically better connection than you can just by soldering the lead to one side of the connector blade. I tin the wire and the blade, and then I use a Dremel tool with a fiber cut-off disc to slot the tinned end of the wire. Be sure that the slot is slightly shorter than the connector blade and that you fully engage the two components before you solder them. This technique doubles the effective solder area and gives a much stronger joint. As always, finish by insulating the solder joint using heat-shrink tubing.

SHOP-MADE BANANA JACKS

I wanted to install a balancer between my charger and LiPo battery, and I needed banana jacks for the charger to receive the plugs on the balancer. Naturally, I didn't have any jacks lying around. I added extra leads to the charger with the homemade banana jacks, as shown. Use approximately 1 inch of K&S $^3/_{16}$-inch-diameter brass tube (no. 129), and insert a nail or a drill-bit shank to avoid deforming the tube when you crimp the end flat. Drill a $^1/_{16}$ hole and solder the lead wire; smooth the sharp corners with a file, and cover the assembly with heat-shrink tubing. You now have a small in-line banana jack that's well insulated, barely larger than the wire and cost only a few cents.

Build a Parallel Wire Harness for Small LiPo Batteries

Increase capacity and discharge rate

by Tom Atwood

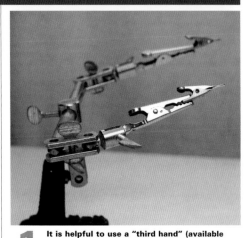

1 It is helpful to use a "third hand" (available from RadioShack) with alligator clips to hold the leads and connectors when you solder. Note the small, toothless copper alligator clips that hold the wire leads and connectors.

The completed harness with two Thunder Power batteries connected in parallel. The Power Pole connectors will connect the harness to the speed control.

L ithium Polymer (LiPo) batteries have revolutionized electric flight by packing more energy into a smaller, lighter package than can be achieved with Ni-Cd and NiMH batteries. LiPo batteries are improving steadily, and the newest cells offer higher discharge rates than previous generations.

Here, we show you how to build a simple parallel wire harness that will enable you to wire two small LiPo packs in parallel for use in a small sport model. This technique works with any LiPo battery type and gives you the dual benefits of increased capacity and a higher discharge rate.

BEFORE ASSEMBLY

The recommended maximum discharge rate for a LiPo battery is characterized as a multiple of the cell's capacity. The Thunder Power 11.1V packs shown are 830mAh 3S packs; they are made up of three 830mAh cells wired in series. This battery can deliver current at an 8.5C discharge rate. If you multiply the rated capacity of 830mAh by 8.5, you can see that this 3S pack is capable of providing 7 amps of current (8.5x0.83Ah = current ceiling of 7 amps).

If you wire two of these packs in parallel, the voltage remains at 11.1 but total battery capacity increases to 1660mAh (twice 830mAh). This 3S2P pack (3 cells in series, two blocks of these in parallel) can deliver 8.5x1.66Ah = 14 amps of current. With a parallel wire harness, you can easily separate the two packs for individual charging, which is recommended.

The small polarized Deans connectors that connect the harness to the batteries are individually rated up to 15 amps and can easily handle the current this pack will provide. The DuraTrax Power Pole connectors easily handle up to 60 amps. When making a harness, make sure that the connectors and the wire gauge are suitable for the current loads you expect.

5 A special tool is available to help seat the Power Pole pin in the connector housing. A small flat-head screwdriver also works well.

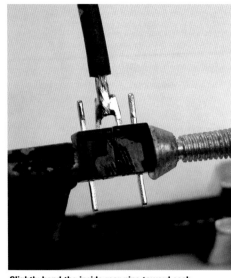

Slightly bend the inside rear pins toward each other to facilitate soldering the positive lead to both.

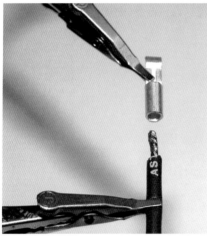

2 When soldering Power Pole connectors, first tin the wire that is to be inserted into the connector pin pocket.

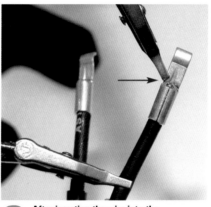

3 After inserting the wire into the connector, apply a soldering iron or a heat gun to the underside of the connector. Do so until it is hot enough to wick solder into the connector from the opening at the front end of the pocket (next to the tip of the upper alligator clip).

4 The tongue on the end of the Power Pole pin snaps over the metal lip inside the connector housing during installation.

6 The pins protruding from the back of the Deans polarized connectors before and after tinning. Tinning the pins and the wire leads that will be joined to them simplifies soldering.

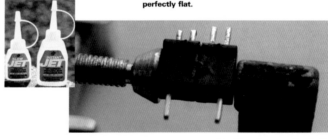

7 Align the two Deans polarized connectors so that their external pins are on the outside. These pins will have negative polarity. Glue the cases together with thin CA. I use a piece of wood to wick a little thin Jet CA onto the case. Before doing this, you may want to lightly file the mating surfaces so that they are perfectly flat.

9 Next, cover the solder joint with heat-shrink and use a heat gun to shrink it into place. To make it easier to solder the negative lead, which must span both outside rear pins, bend the slightly recessed pin (left) forward with a pair of needle-nose pliers. You can also bow the tinned wire at the end of the negative lead.

10 The negative lead has been soldered to the first pin. Because both the wire and the pin were pre-tinned, the solder joint can be created quickly and easily without melting through the heat-shrink that surrounds the positive lead. Next, solder the negative lead to the other outside pin.

11 The last step is to shrink-wrap the connector so that no leads are exposed. I used needle-nose pliers to expand a small section of heat-shrink tubing so that it would easily slip over the connector housing.

THE FINISHED HARNESS

World Championship-Winning 2.4GHz

5 GLOW/GAS POWER ESSENTIALS FOR OPTIMAL PERFORMANCE

For many, few sounds are more inspiring than that of a well-tuned reciprocating engine pulling a model into the sky. To enjoy that experience, it's important to properly break in, tune, install and maintain your mill. Time-tested techniques for glow and gas engines are packed into this chapter. Learn how to stop leaks, store your engines in the shop, mount engines and much more. A feature article on breaking in and tuning by master modeler Andrew Coholic is included.

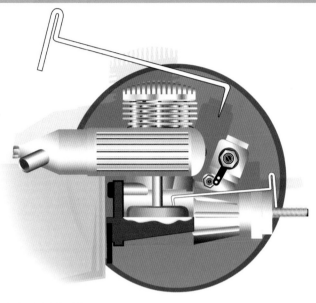

EXTEND YOUR REACH

While installing an engine, I could not get my fingers or needle-nose pliers between the engine mount, the engine and the side of the plane to start the nut and locking washer. I dropped them several times before I found that I could put the nut and locking washer on the end of my magnetic pick-up tool, fit it into the small space and put them perfectly on the end of the bolt. The magnet held the nut so that I could start the bolt from below. Then I just pulled the magnet away and finished tightening the bolt with a small wrench. This made easy work out of an almost impossible and very frustrating job.

MARK ENGINE MOUNTS

Here is a simple technique for getting all four holes properly aligned in a new engine mount. Simply paint the mount beams with Wite-Out or another correction fluid. Once it has dried, bend the tip of a standard T-pin over at 90 degrees, and scribe the inside of the mounting holes. Remove the motor, mark the centers, and drill four perfectly positioned holes.

MULTICOLORED TANK LINES

When putting a multi-line fuel-tank assembly together, I use colored lines to mark the fill, carb and pressure lines. I cut 2mm slices of colored fuel tubing and slide it onto the appropriate fuel fitting. If I need to, I put a slightly longer piece of brass tube through the cap to accommodate the extra line marker. My convention is blue to the carb, red to the exhaust pressure tap and green for filling and emptying (with short tubing and a clunk that sits toward the center of the tank). Continually detaching the carb line is an invitation for a leak. The colored rings make it clear which line is which, so when you install the tank, there is no chance that you'll put the carb line on the pressure line, etc. For the installation, just slide the fuel line up to the marker. The alternative is to spend 10 minutes holding the tank up to a bright light at the field only to discover that you guessed wrong. Look in the nitro car section at the hobby store for colored fuel line.

TEST-STAND PROP CAGE

I've never been really comfortable with the spinning prop while bench-testing my engines. It is one thing on the plane at the field where I know it will only be next to me for a short time but quite another thing on the test bench. How can I test safely without losing a finger or just spoiling my day? A $15 household electric fan-blade cage was the answer. Mount the cage on your bench. Also, the front can be included for extra safety. Remove the Logo plate to allow access to your starter, and Dremel out a few sections of wire in front of the cylinder to improve the airflow.

FUEL DOTS

A lifetime of modeling has trained me to never throw anything away because it might come in handy. I'm a diabetic, and the packaging for the covers of the lances I use with an insulin pen have many uses for glow fliers; I've supplied my club mates with them for years. Unmodified, they fit medium and large fuel tubing and make great fuel dots. Trim off the narrow end, and glue it into a small hole in the fuselage side or the cowl to make a neat vent for your overflow line. Trim two covers and epoxy their flanges together; the resulting part makes a great bulkhead fitting for running the fuel line from the tank to the carburetor. Cut both ends, and use as a joiner for short sections of fuel tubing. Electric modelers can use them as well. Trim the end of a cover off, and mount it in the fuselage as a neat antenna exit. They also make great wheel bushings for park flyers with thin wire gear.

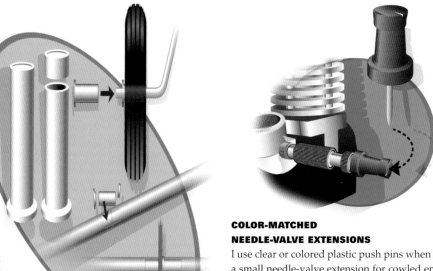

COLOR-MATCHED NEEDLE-VALVE EXTENSIONS

I use clear or colored plastic push pins when I need a small needle-valve extension for cowled engines. I notch the head of the pin to give an indication mark, and then just slide it into the hole in the needle valve. Usually, they are a press-fit and hold securely. The colored tack blends into the color of the cowl and looks great.

END ENGINE LEAKS

Any engine will run cleaner and better if you take the time to properly seal it. Buy high-temperature sealant such as Permatex High-Temp Red RTV Silicone Gasket Maker and apply it very sparingly to any metal-to-metal surfaces where hot gases and oil might leak out. Here, sealant is applied between the exhaust flange and the manifold. Apply just enough so that you can see a tiny amount extrude as the parts are bolted down. This will form a tiny gasket that will keep the goo coming out the muffler, where it is supposed to exit.

PLUG YOUR CARB

If you hang your glow models by the tail, you know that fuel and oil can drip from the carburetor during storage. Foam earplugs solve this nicely, keeping dust and dirt out, while keeping the oil in. They make a snug fit, and hold well. Just squeeze the end and push them into place at the end of the day.

VACUUM-BAG ENGINES FOR STORAGE

If you are like most modelers, you have more engines than planes to use them with. This calls for good storage. Until recently, I relied on Ziploc bags. I'd suck out all the air I could and then finish sealing the bag. Then we bought a vacuum sealing machine for the kitchen. It's a workshop tool! Oil your engine well, particularly the carburetor, and then place it in a sealing bag and put it into the machine. The device evacuates the bag better than I ever could and then seals it in a bag with no air to let it rust. These machines are now so inexpensive that you could actually buy another one for your kitchen. I worry about my stored engines much less now than ever before.

ORIENT THE ENGINE HEAD

If your engine has a symmetrical cooling head and you have removed it to service your engine, it's best to remount the head in its original orientation. This is because microscopic asymmetries in the head's original position can affect the piston wear during break-in. If you remount the head with its front rotated, the alignment and piston pinch will not be precisely the same. Use an X-Acto blade to scratch a small "X" on the front of the head; this will guarantee that you'll correctly align it when you bolt it back onto the crankcase. Also remember to cross-tighten the bolts as if you are tightening lug nuts on a car wheel. You can tell when the head is perfectly mounted by turning the prop with your hand; it will offer the least resistance when the head is perfectly seated.

NO-BURR TUBE CUTTING

The K&S tube cutter does a great job, but it always squeezes the tube a little and leaves a burr on the inside. Instead of trying to ream the cut end later, I insert a piece of music wire of the appropriate size into the tube as a shim before I cut. Put a little lube, either oil or petroleum jelly, on the music wire first to make it easier to remove when you've finished cutting. With this technique, I no longer have problems with burrs or partially crushed tubes.

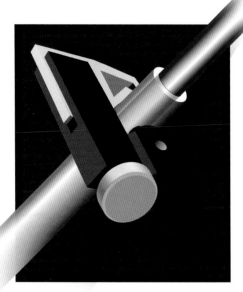

THOROUGH CLEANING

After a crash, I sometimes find it hard to get all the dirt off the engine so that I can inspect it for cracks and other damage that might prevent it from running reliably later. I discovered that a fingernail brush works well to clean engines. With a little warm water and soap, these brushes work quite well for getting into hard to reach places such as those between cooling fins.

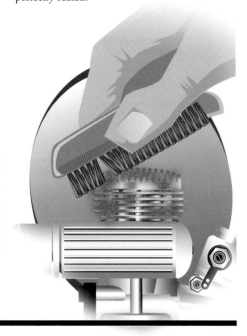

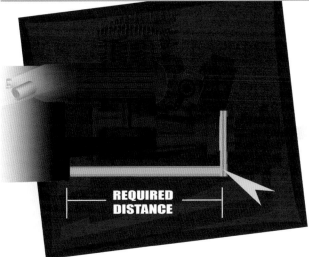

ENGINE-MOUNTING STANDOFF

I discovered an easy way to set the distance of an engine from the firewall. I was building a Hanger 9 Twist, and it called for the engine to be 4.25 inches off the firewall. I built a jig that is connected to the engine as a prop would be. The template has two scrap balsa arms that are cut to the required length and hold the engine in the right spot. I use a rubber band to hold the engine, leaving my hands free to mark the engine mount for drilling.

FUEL-LINE SUPPORT

Have you ever nosed a model over to a sudden stop on a not-so-nice landing? We all have. When you retrieve your plane, everything works fine, so you fill up and take off again. In a minute or so, the engine quits—deadstick. You bring it back, check the engine, top it off and take off again, only to have another deadstick a minute or two later. On that hard landing, the clunk weight probably came forwards and got stuck in the upper front of the fuel tank. Go to your local Seven-11 and get a Slurpee straw. These fit over fuel tubing perfectly. Cut a piece that's long enough to go from the front of the fuel tank to just short of the clunk. This will allow the clunk to move freely in the tank, but it will prevent it from ever flipping again.

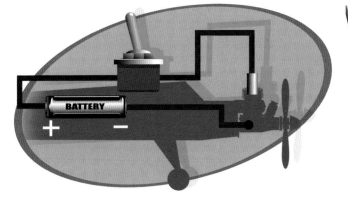

ONBOARD IGNITION

I use a simple onboard ignition source to start my glow engines safely. You'll need an AA battery holder and a toggle switch, a rechargeable battery and a head-lock connector for the glow plug. Wire the model as shown, and then turn the switch on to start the engine; turn it off as soon as the engine is running. This works great and keeps your fingers away from the spinning prop. If you need power at the field, you can even put an alkaline battery in the holder.

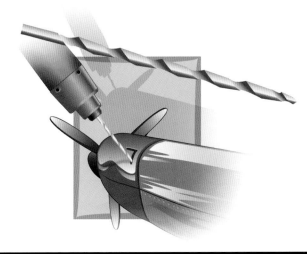

CLEAN COWL TRIMMING

This will improve your life when you cut cowl holes. Use a side-cutting spiral bit that's commonly used by drywall professionals. This same inexpensive bit can be used in a Dremel tool and will cut holes in any plastic or fiberglass cowls as easily as a hot knife cuts butter. It leaves such a clean cut that hardly any sanding is needed. Determine where the hole should be and draw its outline using a marker. Simply set the Dremel tool to high speed, and push the bit into the cowl on the marked line; then carefully guide it along the line. A little light sanding with 220-grit sandpaper will give the cut edge a perfectly professional look. The side-cutting bit doesn't make the cracks you get when you cut with a saw blade that requires an up/down motion.

Break in & tune
your model engines

The keys to glow-power success

Photos and story by Andrew Coholic

For many of the newest participants in our hobby (and even for many who have been modeling for some time), the idea of and procedures for proper engine "break-in" can be confusing. With many different ideas about the best way to break in our model airplane engines on the Internet, being discussed at our flying clubs and appearing in publications, you're undoubtedly wondering how to run and tune the various model engines safely. As with so many other aspects of this hobby, you can use various methods to achieve the same result. Here, I discuss what I do, as it has worked well for me over the years that I have been buying, running and flying with engines successfully.

ENGINE BREAK-IN

I actually prefer to call it "running in" an engine. Breaking is exactly what you do not want to do! When an engine is manufactured, even with many manufacturers using the latest computer-driven machinery and the most modern tooling, the metal surfaces are still covered in microscopic ridges and machine marks. If you take a brand-new engine, disassemble it and then view the surfaces with a magnifying glass, you'll actually see the machine marks. Other parts of the engine may have microscopic burrs along the edges, and others (such as sleeves and pistons) may be ever so slightly out of round.

The running-in process is when all of these mating surfaces work against one another while the engine is running. These mating surfaces include the piston and liner, wristpin, piston and connecting rod, crankshaft and bushings, etc. These parts heat up during break-in and must be given adequate lubrication and cooling from the fuel during it. It is very important that the engine doesn't get too hot and that it's adequately lubricated. During this period, the oil in the fuel acts as a "cushion" between the metal surfaces, and it removes excess heat and carries away the microscopic metal particles that are being worn away from the mating surfaces. I will discuss the requirements of oil later on.

Some engines require a longer break-in than others. Some are sold as needing no break-in or very little. Depending on the materials used, the tolerances and the type of engine, the break-in period can range from as little as a tank of fuel and 10 minutes of running to many gallons and running for hours. In the end, improperly run-in engines can suffer from many problems—most notably, quitting in the air and having poor idle/transition characteristics. All these can lead to the loss of your airframe and a greatly reduced life of the engine.

ENGINE TYPES & WHY IT MATTERS

Today, there are two main types of piston/liner design in use: the first is the ringed style. This usually consists of an aluminum piston with a single expansion ring

running in a hardened- or plated-steel liner. The second is the modern "ABC," or lapped type (excluding the older iron/steel cylinder and piston engines that are not very common today), which can be an aluminum piston running in a chrome or nickel-plated brass liner, although some manufacturers use or offer an aluminum sleeve (also chrome-plated as the brass sleeve would be).

"ABN" refers to the use of a nickel-plated brass sleeve, while "AAC" refers to the aluminum sleeve that has been chrome-plated. In all cases, the piston is made of a high-silicon-content aluminum alloy that has a low coefficient of expansion.

There is a major difference between the run-in procedures for these two main types of engine. Let's deal with each in turn.

FUEL & OIL
WHAT'S RIGHT FOR YOUR ENGINE?

There are many opinions about which is the "best" fuel to run in a modern engine—the nitro percentage to use, the oil percentage and whether or not to use castor or synthetic oil or a blend of the two.

You should aim to break in an engine with the fuel that you intend to run it with afterwards (or something very close to it). With rare exceptions, any modern ABC-type or ringed type of engine will happily be broken in and run on 5%, 10%, or 15% nitro fuel (there isn't a huge difference between 5 and 15%) and an oil content of 18%. (Exception: with certain high-performance engines, you should always use exactly what the manufacturers recommend.) A fuel such as Wildcat Premium Extra —18% oil with a 20:80 castor/synthetic blend—will be more than adequate for the initial runs and general operation later on. The common backyard practice of adding oil to fuel to boost its total percentage is not necessary; again, this applies to ABC-type and ringed type sport engines only. Older lapped steel/iron engines such as the Fox .35 need more oil—from 22% to 26% or even 28%. Some specialty racing engines also need a very specific oil percentage. I assume that if you run these special engines, you already have the experience to operate them properly.

All the major brands of sport engines need no more than 18%; and all the major brands I am aware of specify 18% as being safe to run and enough to meet their respective warranties. As for the oil type, it is always a good idea to run some castor oil in the fuel, especially if you aren't as careful (or you lack the

experience) when you set you engines. One lean run with 100% synthetic oil can spell disaster. Having some castor oil in the fuel will protect the engine in the event of an extremely lean run and if the engine overheats.

The castor oil is superior not only in its lubricating properties but also for carrying away excess heat. The castor oil will break down and form a varnish on the cylinder and piston that will protect them from further damage. The synthetics will burn up and won't protect the precious surfaces of the engine interior. That said, if you have the experience and never run your engines lean, you could safely run 100% synthetic oil. But why take that chance?

PROPELLER SELECTION

For running in an engine, you want a propeller that is slightly less of a load than you will use for flight. For example, the average .46c.i. engine would use a 10x7 or 11x6 prop for flight. A 10x6 or 11x5 would be a good choice for the break-in runs. The lighter load allows the engine to maintain the necessary rpm without overheating. This is not the time to lug down the engine with too much prop!

BREAKING IN
RINGED ENGINES

With ringed engines, the steel sleeve is generally hardened or sometimes chrome-plated. The piston ring is made of ductile iron and then hardened to give it the springiness to press against the cylinder wall and create a gas-tight seal. Since there is some variance in manufacturing processes, the ring and sleeve may not be perfectly round.

The ring needs to "seat" itself with the sleeve—essentially, wearing away until it achieves a nearly perfect fit in the cylinder bore. During initial runs, it is very important that the engine warm up to nearly normal operating temperatures yet also stay on the cooler side to prevent the parts from working against one another to create excess heat. If the engine is allowed to get excessively hot, the oil can break down and cause the metal parts to wear excessively, galling and scratching up the mating surfaces. You can also damage the ring with excessive heating and inadequate cooling caused by a lack of oil (in a lean running condition).

The proper method is to start the engine with the high-speed needle turned out to allow the engine to run very rich. On most

This O.S. LA65 uses an air-bleed carb with a remote high speed needle mounted at the aft end of the crankcase.

The VMAX .46 uses a 2-needle metering carb.

engines, four to five 360-degree turns out from fully closed will do nicely. Remember that you can't hurt the engine by starting too rich, but starting in a lean condition can cause damage!

Once the engine is running, open the carburetor fully, and slowly close the needle until the engine is running in a quick 4-cycle—"4-stroking," as it is called—and if you need to leave the glow igniter on during these rich runs, that's fine. You can tell because the pitch of the sound will drop from an even note that's characteristic of 2-stroking to a much lower pitch. The engine is running steadily, but the sound has an uneven quality, and excessive fuel will drip from the muffler. Run the engine for one to two minutes, and then close the carb to shut it off. Let it cool down for five minutes or so and repeat the procedure half a dozen times.

After this series of initial runs, you can

increase the run time to three to five minutes and, at the same time, slowly lean the needle to a point at which the engine is breaking from "2-stroking" to "4-stroking" on successive runs. Once you have 30 to 40 minutes on the engine, it is time to lean it for a clean 2-stroke setting; see whether it will hold this wide open without sagging. If the engine drops in rpm (you'll hear it), open the needle slightly and allow it to run in longer at a reduced rpm.

When setting the top end, you should always stay 200 or 300rpm below the absolute peak rpm that the engine will turn. You can generally count on the average ringed engine taking at least an hour of carefully controlled

A VMAX .46 is run on the test stand. RCATS system sensors monitor exhaust and head temperature as well as rpm.

running to break in enough to provide reliable performance in all rpm ranges. Some of the larger engines may take a few hours or more. You cannot rush the process, and a little patience now will reward you with a great running engine.

ABC-TYPE ENGINE BREAK-IN

Unlike the ringed engine, the lapped aluminum piston engines are fitted so that the piston becomes tight at the top. This interference fit is necessary for the proper running clearances once the sleeve, the piston and the rest of the engine are up to running temperature; this is why the break-in procedure differs from that for the ringed type.

ABC-type engines require the cylinder to expand to the proper "running fit." Doing this requires that the engine come up to around 300 degrees F. Running in a 'too-cool' state will cause the piston and liner to remain in overly tight and will put excess strain on the connecting rod, the crankpin and the wristpin and will rapidly wear the piston crown. Therefore, on starting a lapped engine, open the throttle

fully and lean the high-speed needle out to a point at which the engine is not in an overly rich state but in a clean, rich 2-cycle.

Run the engine for a minute or two, and then stop it by closing off the carb and allow it to cool. Repeat this half a dozen times. Next, run the engine (again wide open) another half a dozen times, but extend the run time to three to four-minute intervals followed by a cool-down. You can lean the engine slightly on each run, being careful to listen for any tendency to sag (reduction in rpm). If the engine does not hold the setting, open the needle to the point at which it will hold a steady rpm.

After these runs, you should be near the optimum position—approximately 300rpm off the peak. Most ABC-type engines require 30 to 40 minutes of run time to be broken in well enough to be mounted and flown in an aircraft. Some engine manufacturers fit their engines relatively loosely, and these engines will not require as much break-in time. Others fit their pistons quite tightly; these require an additional half an hour's running before the engines will operate smoothly and idle reliably.

The main thing to remember is that under no circumstances should you run the engine in an excessively rich (4-stroking) manner, and do not run at any setting other than wide open. Running at reduced throttle settings will prevent the engine from coming up to the proper temperatures.

2-STROKE VS. 4-STROKE

The procedure for breaking in 2-stoke and 4-stroke engines is the same, and with both types now available in ringed and lapped varieties, just follow the respective break-in procedures.

It is a little more difficult to hear rpm changes in 4-stroke engines because of their lower exhaust notes. I suggest that you use a good tachometer to set rpm, and make sure that the engine is not set at the absolute peak or even too lean. Even for 2-stroke engines, using a tachometer is a good idea.

GENERAL TUNING FOR SPORT ENGINES

Tuning an engine for proper flight performance is not difficult, but it must be done carefully to avoid damaging the engine or having less than ideal running characteristics.

Most 2- and 4-stroke glow engines come with one of two carburetor types: the 2-needle variety or the air-bleed type. There has always been a lot of controversy as to which carb style is better. The more expensive engines usually

come with the 2-needle type, but I've found that most engines will idle and transition just fine with their provided air-bleed carburetors if set up properly.

When tuning an engine, I usually start with the main needle (high-speed needle) out at least four or five 360-degree turns, or in accordance with the recommendations given in the operating instructions. But I have bought engines that had to be opened up to three turns more than what was recommended.

Don't be scared to start the engine rich; it won't hurt it! Starting too lean, on the other hand, is not good. Once the engine has been started—and with the glow igniter still attached; do not be quick to remove it—open the carb fully and start leaning out the high-speed needle. With a broken in engine (any style), you should use a tachometer and keep leaning until a gain in rpm is no longer produced with any additional leaning of the needle. Then back off at least 200rpm and preferably 300rpm or even 400rpm from the peak.

Of course, this all depends on the engine, prop and fuel combo you run and in which kind of airframe. Avoid having the engine unload in the air and possibly leaning out too much and overheating. Running a little on the rich side will prevent this from happening.

TRICKS OF THE TRADE

Some tricks to help with engine tuning (for wide-open running) are also easy to do.

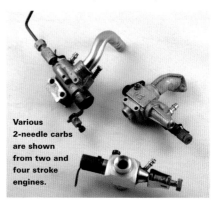

Various 2-needle carbs are shown from two and four stroke engines.

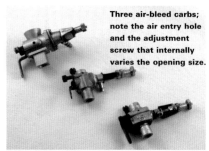

Three air-bleed carbs; note the air entry hole and the adjustment screw that internally varies the opening size.

The "pinch test" will tell you whether the engine is running at peak or not. While it's running, quickly pinch the fuel tubing that goes to the carb and then let go. If the engine rpm increase briefly (watch the tach ,or listen to the exhaust note) and then settle back down, lean the setting out a little more until the pinching doesn't produce this rise in rpm. At this point, back off the needle by approximately $1/4$ turn or 300 to 400rpm, and you are set to go.

Another test involves holding the airplane vertical to check for possible leaning out when the engine has to pull fuel in a climb. You should be able to lift the aircraft's nose to vertical without the engine's leaning out past its peak. Keep adjusting the needle to the point at which the engine doesn't lean out too much when the nose is raised.

Remember, all modern lapped aluminum piston engines have to be run in a clean 2-stroke mode and not excessively rich. If you have access to a temperature gun, the head temperature at the glow plug should be at least 300 to 350 degrees F. On the other hand, a ringed engine can be run richer (cooler) without risk of damage.

One real-life example of how an engine can be ruined comes to mind. A trainer equipped with an ABN-type .40-size engine was being run excessively rich to keep the speed down at full throttle. In a short season of flying, the engine's piston/liner fit was worn to the point at which there was no measurable compression! If you want to limit your plane's speed, simply reduce the throttle. An excessively rich setting is not the proper way to do it.

CARB SETUP

For many modelers, the low-speed setting seems to be the most difficult to set up properly. Let's deal with each type of carb separately.
Air-bleed carbs The air-bleed carburetor relies on a small hole drilled through the carb body to allow air into the engine when the throttle barrel is nearly closed. If the air-bleed hole was not there, the engine would load up with fuel and die. This small hole lets enough air into the engine to lean out the air/fuel mixture enough to keep the engine running.

There is a screw to adjust the opening: screwing it in (clockwise) closes the hole and richens the idle mixture; unscrewing the air-bleed screw (counterclockwise) allows more air to enter the carb and thus leans the mix-

ture. To adjust this, simply bring the engine down to idle (after it has been running for at least 30 seconds to make sure it has warmed up) and listen. If the engine slowly dies and then quits, it is being run too rich and is overloading

Left: an O.S. air-bleed carb. Right: this 2-needle carb has a low-speed (idle) adjustment screw inside the throttle-arm assembly.

The low-speed adjustment needle on a Vmax .46 engine (distributed by Richmond RC) is within the barrel opposite the high-speed (main) needle. Many engines use this configuration.

with fuel. Open the air-bleed screw a little and try it again. If the engine runs for a few seconds and quits, it is probably too lean, and the adjustment screw has to be closed a little.

When you can idle the engine steadily, check the transition. If you open the carb and the engine stutters and hesitates before it picks up in rpm, it is running too rich. If it starts to accelerate and stops quickly, it is too lean; adjust the air-bleed screw to compensate. You should be able to get a decent idle and transition from most engines using an air-bleed carb; they may be some slight hesitation when quickly accelerating from a prolonged idle, but the engine should never quit.

Two-needle metering carb The 2-needle, or metering, carb actually alters the volume of fuel that's allowed to pass through it when the throttle barrel is closed. In some carbs, a secondary needle enters via the end of the spray bar to meter the fuel, and you'll find various other forms of metering in other carbs. The main thing to remember is that you are actually varying how much fuel is allowed into the engine (unlike the air-bleed carb). It can be a more precise way to achieve an excellent idle and transition.

In the 2-needle carb, the low-speed needle can affect the engine at settings other than idle. If the idle needle is set too lean, it can actually cause the engine to run lean at higher throttle settings as well (the amount varies according to carb design).

To set the idle and transition, lean it (turn the low-speed needle clockwise) until the

engine idles cleanly without loading up with fuel and dying. Transitioning from idle should be clean and without sputtering; lean out the low-speed adjustment needle and repeat until the engine can be throttled up cleanly.

Conversely, if the engine dies abruptly when you advance the throttle, the low-speed needle is set too lean and needs to be opened. Make small adjustments–perhaps $1/8$ turn at a time; restart the engine and try again. Once the low-speed needle has been set, recheck the high-speed (wide-open) running and readjust the main needle valve if necessary.

Setting the needles on any model engine is not difficult, but you need to approach it with an understanding of how the various needles and adjustments affect performance. Adjust one thing at a time in a small way, and do not excessively screw the needles in and out without reason. Sometimes, a very small adjustment makes a world of difference to an engine's performance. Go slowly!

WRAP-UP

Most of the engines sold today come with very thorough operating instructions. It is always a good idea to start with the recommended fuel, prop, etc. As you gain experience and understanding by running more and more engines, you will enhance your skills to the point at which setting up and running your engine is easy and even pleasurable.

Author's note: I am indebted to the following engine authorities who have written extensively in the modeling press for many years: David Gierke, Clarence Lee, Peter Chinn and Mike Billinton. I have studied their work extensively, and there is no doubt that I have incorporated much of their wisdom and many of their techniques into my own approaches to engine break-in, tuning and testing. It is not possible for me to document which tip I picked up from which author and when, but I do express my heartfelt thanks to these mentors for pioneering the way for the rest of us. ✪

 AT THE FLYING FIELD

Transporting your model to the flying field, setting it up on the bench, quickly addressing practical issues to get your ship into the air and other "hands on" field-related techniques are included in this chapter. There is nothing like a customized field stand that holds and protects your model. See our feature article on building your own!

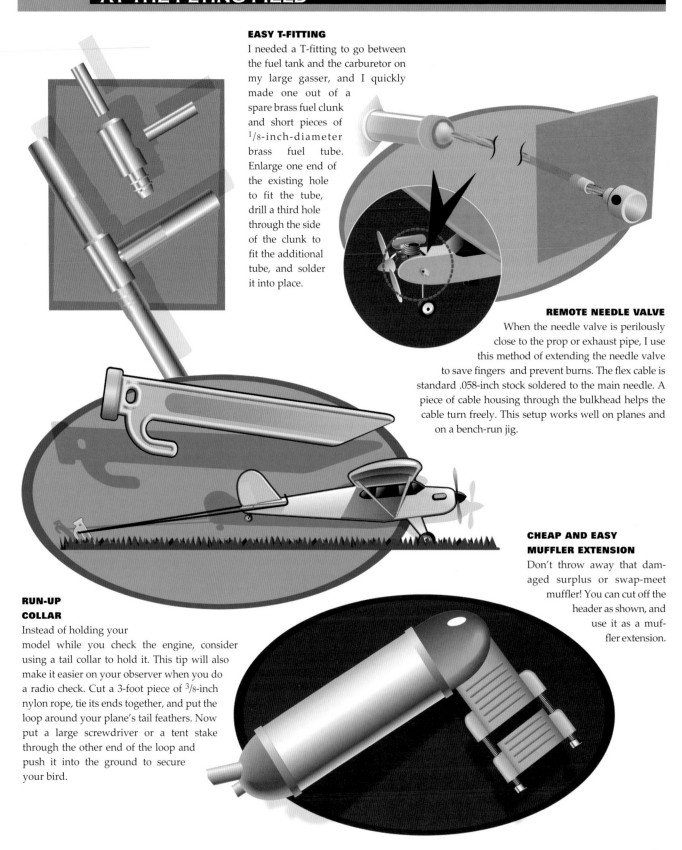

EASY T-FITTING

I needed a T-fitting to go between the fuel tank and the carburetor on my large gasser, and I quickly made one out of a spare brass fuel clunk and short pieces of $1/8$-inch-diameter brass fuel tube. Enlarge one end of the existing hole to fit the tube, drill a third hole through the side of the clunk to fit the additional tube, and solder it into place.

REMOTE NEEDLE VALVE

When the needle valve is perilously close to the prop or exhaust pipe, I use this method of extending the needle valve to save fingers and prevent burns. The flex cable is standard .058-inch stock soldered to the main needle. A piece of cable housing through the bulkhead helps the cable turn freely. This setup works well on planes and on a bench-run jig.

CHEAP AND EASY MUFFLER EXTENSION

Don't throw away that damaged surplus or swap-meet muffler! You can cut off the header as shown, and use it as a muffler extension.

RUN-UP COLLAR

Instead of holding your model while you check the engine, consider using a tail collar to hold it. This tip will also make it easier on your observer when you do a radio check. Cut a 3-foot piece of $3/8$-inch nylon rope, tie its ends together, and put the loop around your plane's tail feathers. Now put a large screwdriver or a tent stake through the other end of the loop and push it into the ground to secure your bird.

FREE PADDED CHICKEN STICKS

I recently found a great idea for making a chicken stick while cleaning out my garage. I cut the handles off a few broken fishing poles. The handles make great chicken sticks with foam padding that are about a foot long. Mine now sports a few cuts in the foam from nasty backfires, but better the foam than my fingers!

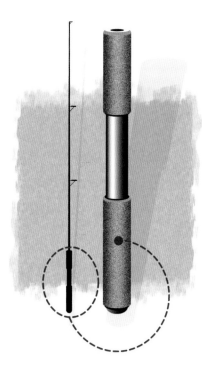

AFFORDABLE FOLDING FIELD BENCH

I wanted a solid field bench for my first gas plane, yet didn't want to pay the advertised price of the wooden benches. When I saw this Stanley Folding Workbench at a home-supply store, I thought it would make a great field bench. I also picked up a piece of PVC pipe, a few fittings, and some foam pipe insulation to make a fuselage cradle. I think this bench is tougher and lighter than the wooden ones, and for only $30, it was a bargain. You can also use it for other projects around the house or shop.

BREAK-IN MODEL HOLDER

After searching in vain for a model hold-down that would keep my model off the ground while I broke in my new engine in clean air, I decided to build my own. I drilled a couple of 1-inch holes centered 10.5 inches from either end of a 28-inch-long 2x6. I drilled the holes at approximately a 10-degree angle from vertical and cut two 15-inch lengths of dowel and epoxied them into the holes. Next, I cut two equal lengths of foam pipe insulation; I glued this foam around the dowels and then trimmed it to fit. Finally, I glued two PVC caps on top of the dowels and pipe insulation for a neat finished look. The 2x6 is 28 inches long because that's the width of my picnic table. I clamp it to both sides of the table and can tune and break in my new engines without having to kneel.

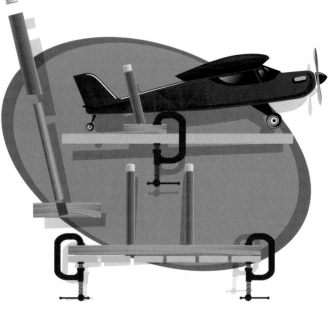

SAFE TRANSPORT

I have been using this wheel chock system since 1984 to transport everything from trainers up to giant scale models. I cut a 3/4-inch plywood panel to fit the back of my SUV and use wood screws to attach large tuna fish cans, spaced for a particular model. I also install a small bungee cord, to flip over the wheels and hold them in the cans. This system has held fast even on the occasional panic stop, with no damage to my models or vehicle.

COOLER MODEL STORAGE

I have several park flyers and recently hit on this idea for easy transportation and convenient storage for them. I bought a cheap foam cooler and notched the sides to accept the wings with the models positioned nose-down. If you make the notches just deep enough, the bottom of the cooler offers a convenient place to carry your transmitter, extra batteries, or other accessories.

LITHIUM CHARGER LEADS

A number of the new lithium chargers have banana plug leads to which you solder your connector(s) of choice. Because different lithium packs of different capacities come wired with any of several types of connectors, solder additional connector types to the banana jacks so that your charger output leads match the connectors on your packs—eliminating the need for additional patch cords. Just one hint: avoid mounting multiple connector output leads if more than one connector type has protruding pins (to safeguard against shorts).

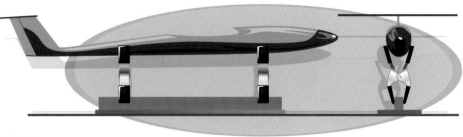

SOFT-SIDED FIELD BOX

It seems like it is always a challenge to organize all the bits and pieces we need while flying. I made a nice little field "box" for my Speed 400 and smaller planes using a soft-sided 6-pack type cooler. I'm able to fit a 7Ah sealed, lead-acid battery, my charger, and several 8-cell $^2/3$A size packs in the main compartment with room to spare. My cooler also has a couple of outside pockets I use for CA, scissors, tape, spare props, tools, etc.

SIMPLE SKINNY-FUSELAGE STAND

I've found a simple, effective way to park those skinny glider and hot-liner fuselages and greatly reduce the risk of damaging their fragile V-tails, T-tails, etc. This is very handy on the workbench, at the field and when you transport your aircraft. You need several pieces of wood and at least two clamps. Measure the length of the fuselage and cut your stand base accordingly. For extra protection, I usually add foam where the clamp handles meet. Add "feet" to the base to make the stand easy to pick up.

SIMPLE FIELD STAND & TOOL BOX

I have a few old Styrofoam coolers in the garage. Instead of buying a commercial plane stand, just cut a few U-shape grooves in the top of the cooler sides. You can cut grooves on all four sides so both larger and smaller planes fit. Such a stand is great. It's very cheap, and if you tend to drop those little fiddly parts while working on a plane, they'll probably fall into the cooler. When you go flying, just throw in your supplies to carry them all to the field.

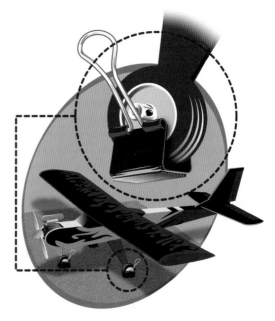

SIMPLE CHOCKS FOR LIGHTWEIGHT MODELS

I have been searching for a way to prevent my park flyers from getting dinged up when rolling around in the back of my SUV. I tried several types of wheel chocks with varied success. One day, I came across some large binder clips in my desk, and a winning idea occurred to me. I put the hook side of some sticky-backed Velcro on the bottom of the clips and then clipped them to my aircraft's wheels. The hooks grab the carpeting in my vehicle securely and keep my models stationary. No more damage when transporting airplanes! The cost? $1.95 for a dozen clips. I had the Velcro in my box.

CUSTOM HELICOPTER WORK STAND

Lego and Duplo plastic building bricks can be used to make a stand that you can use while doing maintenance and modifying the underside of a micro-helicopter. The simple pillar design shown will let you support the helicopter upside-down by its skids with the rotors out of harm's way.

Build a Custom PVC Stand to protect your model

by Jack J. Joseph

Once I finish building an airplane, I immediately build a stand for it. Why? Because such a stand stabilizes the fuselage and makes it easy to attach the wing, or connect the servo wires, etc., and it also protects the plane from your workbench. Whenever you set a fuselage down anywhere, you invite problems. When the fuselage lies inverted, the fin and rudder, the canopy and cowl and the glow plug are stressed as you jiggle the plane around while you prepare it for flight. An inexpensive, easy-to-make PVC pipe stand eliminates the chance of your having these problems.

Here's how to make a custom stand:

1. Make a rough sketch of your proposed stand. If you can't draw, do the best you can, or follow photo 3 as a guide.

2. Determine the correct length of your stand by deciding where you want the fuselage to rest on it and then measuring that distance. I like my stands to fit the fuselage 6 inches in front of the horizontal stabilizer and just in front of the landing gear. In the case of the Banchee, that distance was 26 inches, and that will be the overall length of the Banchee's stand. Make a line sketch to show this.

3. Measure the width of the fuselage where it will rest on the stand. Mark those measurements on your sketch.

4. Use your sketch to determine how many 90-degree elbows, caps and T-pipes you'll need. The Banshee frame required 6 caps, 10 Ts and 4 elbows. You'll also need some $1/2$-inch-diameter PVC pipe (it comes in 10-foot lengths, so you'll have some left over for your next stand), a can of cement and 6 feet of $1/2$-inch-inside-diameter foam pipe insulation. Now head off to a hardware store and buy all these.

1 When you put your airplane down like this, you can expect to damage to the fin and rudder, the canopy and cowl and the glow plug.

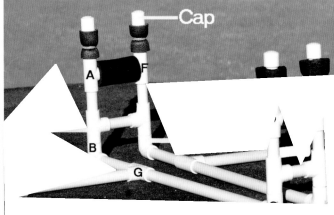

2 Placed in a stand, the airplane is secure and protected from being damaged.

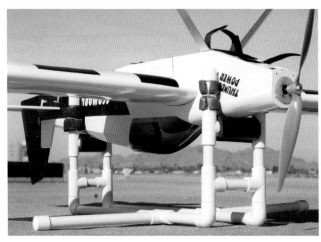

4 Your stand should be high enough to keep the propeller and fin/rudder off the surface when the fuselage is inverted, and the wheels shouldn't touch the surface when the plane is upright.

3 Dimensions for the Banshee stand: A-B—7.5 in.; B-C—26 in.; C-D—7 in., D-E—3 in.; A-F—4 in.; G-H—6 in. (two pieces added to the stand to increase its lateral stability).

5. Make the stand's base. A PVC pipe cutter, will make the job easier, but I cut the pipe with a hacksaw. The cuts do not have to be perfect because they'll be hidden in the various Ts and elbow pieces. Do not glue anything yet.

6. Continue to join the pipes until you have what looks like a stand.

7. Set the stand on your bench, and adjust it until it sits flat and is stable. Mark the joints with a pencil so that you'll be able to match them exactly.

8. Now is the time to glue the joints. The glue sets immediately, so be sure that your pencil marks are aligned when you put the parts together. If the structure is sturdy enough, you may not need to glue it.

9. Add the foam pipe insulation, and you've finished.

You could use other materials to make a stand, but PVC pipe is preferred. Check the photographs of the alternatives. But no matter which material you choose, make a stand and protect your plane from assembly rash.

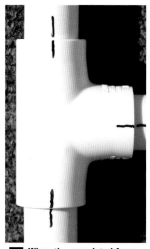

5 When the completed frame is adjusted and sits flat, mark every joint like this.

6 Ollie Edwards added outriggers to his stand to hold the wing for transportation. Note the pipes added to the bottom of the frame to add lateral stability.

8 Quarter-inch plywood, cushioned with rubber pipe insulation was used to make this quick stand. The cutouts for the fuselage can be made to fit any model exactly.

9 Aftermarket stands are available, but I find that they don't match most fuselages and are a bit rickety.

11 An inexpensive Styrofoam cooler with its ends carved out makes a fine but somewhat fragile stand. There's room in the bottom for a few tools.

7 A unique plane holder made using an adjustable bench that's available from the tool section of most chainstores and department stores. The PVC frame fits into holes drilled in the bench's wooden platform.

10 A great stand for modelers with aching backs. Pipe holders were attached to the ends of the flight box. PVC pipes, with cushioned fuselage holders, were cut to the modeler's height and inserted into the pipe holders. They can be removed for transportation.

12 A nice construction but it's unstable. The bottoms of the curved fuselage holders do not match the fuselage's flat bottom. ✪